The Genie Within

Your Subconscious Mind

How It Works
and
How To Use It

Harry W. Carpenter

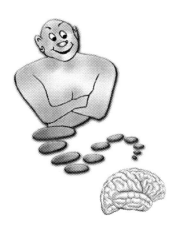

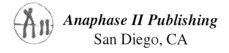

Anaphase II Publishing
San Diego, CA

The Genie Within
Your Subconscious Mind
How It Works and How To Use It

Illustrations by Dale Sutton

Cover Design by Lily Splane (from illustrations by Dale Sutton)
CyberScribe Electronic Document Design
WWW.CYBERLEPSY.COM   LILY@CYBERLEPSY.COM

Cover sky background photo © 2004 Helen Weinman

ISBN 13:   798-0-945962-28-1 (paperback)
ISBN 10:   0-945962-28-2
            0-945962-29-0 (e-book)

WWW.THEGENIEWITHIN.NET

Printed in the United States of America

ANAPHASE II Publishing
2739 Wightman Street
San Diego, CA 92104-3526
WWW.CYBERLEPSY.COM/ANAPHASE.HTM

DISCLAIMER

These lectures are intended for average people who desire to be healthy, stay healthy, become better persons, improve skills, and have peace of mind. These lectures are not meant to replace professional help. The ways you can use this information are limitless and how you use it is up to you. I cannot take responsibility for how you use it. I have no formal training in therapy or medicine. This book does not take the place of competent health professionals. If you have an emotional or physical problem, you should consult a doctor or therapist. Symptoms are not the cause of the problem. Eliminating symptoms without eliminating the cause can be dangerous.

There are relaxation/alpha routines after each lesson. Do not practice these while driving, operating equipment, or any other activity that requires your conscious, critical attention. After the routine is over, be certain that you are wide awake and alert before you resume any activity.

The purpose of this book is to educate. The author and publisher shall have neither liability nor responsibility to any person or entity with respect to any loss or damage caused, or alleged to be caused, directly or indirectly by the information contained in this book.

Dedication

This book is dedicated to my wife, Jane, for her patience, selflessness, and teaching me to appreciate the beauty in nature.

ACKNOWLEDGEMENTS

I wish to thank my friends who read a draft copy and gave me feedback. Four people deserve special consideration: Brett Mitchell, who read a draft before anyone else and gave me the confidence to continue; Lily Splane, who found a zillion of those little errors an author cannot see, and made helpful comments about recent scientific studies; my wife, Jane, who was my *in-house* reviewer, for her patience; and my daughter, Christine Carpenter, who got involved late but, nonetheless, made valuable contributions. My thanks also go to these friends who took time to read all or part of the manuscript and make comments: Elizabeth Roberts, Niki Hale, Roland Behny, Sam Huston, and Pat Sica.

Many thanks to Lily Splane for her effort in designing the cover, and to Helen Weinman for the background photograph of the sky and clouds.

A special thank you is given to Dale Sutton who drew the catchy cartoons that enhance and enliven *The Genie Within*.

I thank the many students in my classes that asked me where they could find one book that contained all the information in my course. Their interest helped prod me into writing *The Genie Within*.

Table of Contents

PREFACE

Tapping the power in the subconscious mind has been my avocation for a long time. What I learned came from reading every book I could find on the subject and from seminars. At the urging of friends, I put together a course consisting of six lessons of two hours each. (The six lessons are extended to eight lessons in this book for convenience.) The course is the distillation of the best of what I learned and used. After every class, students ask where they can buy a book with this information. My answer is that this information was gleaned from many sources and no book comes close to containing all of it. This book, *The Genie Within,* contains all of it.

The only thing that is original to me is putting the information together. I credit the authors of the books I read and two notable seminars, *Psycho-Netics* taught by James Takus, in Tarzana, CA, and an advanced Silva class taught by Burt Goldman. My guess is that in most, if not all cases this information was not original to the authors either. The basic information has been passed on for centuries.

I have read more books on this subject than I can remember. I took some notes but, unfortunately, I did not write down sources. Often the same concept or story appeared in several books. I have included a bibliography of the books that contributed most to my knowledge or are worth reading.

These lessons are not esoteric or metaphysical. They are easy to understand and the techniques are easy to use. This information is basic and should be understood by everyone interested in achieving success and making his or her life better in every way. *The Genie Within* is a "how to" book that

provides concrete ways to achieve goals, change undesirable habits, and more.

For some reason this course has attracted only adults. My goal is to pass this knowledge on to teens and young adults. This information would be invaluable to them for excelling in school, easing the process of growing up, increasing their self-esteem, and enriching their lives. I trust that this book will find that audience.

I recently added a lecture on prayer because prayer is powerful. Unlike the previous lectures, some of the concepts in this lesson *are* mine. They are logical extensions of the first eight lessons. You will not find them in any book that I am aware of. I had qualms about the way some readers might react to such an emotional subject as prayer. But because it is, in my opinion, the most important lesson and it is an invaluable sequel to the first eight lectures, I included it as part of *The Genie Within*.

> *Harry Carpenter*
> Fallbrook, California
> Spring, 2007

PROLOGUE

A Parable

When he was just a boy, the old man heard a story of a woman who found a corked bottle on the beach. When she pulled the cork from the bottle, she imagined a genie came out. The genie granted the women all her wishes. The old man spent his life searching for his own bottle with a genie in it. He combed the beaches of every continent. Because of his obsession, he never made lasting relationships or held a job for long. He was an unhappy man.

One day on a beach near his home, he found the bottle he had been looking for. For a reason unknown to him, he felt there was a genie inside. Corks in other bottles were hard to pull out, but this one slipped out easily. Out of nowhere a genie appeared. The genie said to the old man, "I am here to grant you whatever you want."

"Whatever I want?" replied the old man.

"Well," said the genie," almost anything. Since you are old and have never been in politics, it's unlikely that you can become President of the United States, nor do I think it wise to wish for a spot on the Olympic basketball team. And I do not think you want anything taken at someone else's expense. So, no, not everything. Still, more than you have dreamed of. Certainly enough to make you happy and peaceful."

The old man was ecstatic but then he became angry. "Why has it taken me so long to find you? I could have accomplished so much had I found you when I was young."

"Ah, master" said the genie, "but I have been with you all

along. I was not in that bottle. I have been with you and granting your wishes all of your life. Remember when you were six and you wished your father would pay more attention to you? You cut your finger. That was no accident. Your father washed the cut and held you. Remember? There was the time you took the CPA exam. You kept telling me you were not smart enough to be a CPA and that you were not worthy to make as much money as a CPA. Remember how you froze during the exam? You got your wish."

"Because you were not aware I was granting wishes," continued his genie, "your wishes often hurt you. Sometimes the wishes were not even yours. They came from parents, teachers, friends, and, yes, often from TV ads."

"I am glad you found me. Now you will make wishes that are thoughtful and good. Now we can work together. Together we can stay healthy, find peace, and enjoy the richness of life. But first, I must give you this book. Read it carefully. If you follow these instructions, I will grant you peace, prosperity, and happiness."

"WOW! I didn't know I *already* had one!"

INTRODUCTION

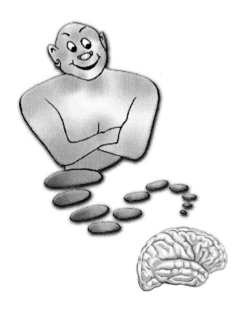

INTRODUCTION

"Your son will probably die, and if by some miracle he lives, he will not be strong enough to get out of bed." I cannot imagine more devastating news for late-in-life parents with only one child. What must have gone through my mom and dad's minds? I was nine years old, in fourth grade, and had been active and athletic.It started one normal afternoon in the fall. I did not feel well but I did not think much of it. I felt worse the next day so my parents took me to our family doctor. He could not determine what was wrong other than it was my heart. I deteriorated so fast that I was sent to the Swedish Covenant Hospital in Chicago where the top cardiologists examined me. The diagnosis was a rare heart condition and there was no cure. That's when they gave my parents the dire news. My mom and dad took me home. Over the next year, I languished in bed at home in and out of consciousness. I was weak and emaciated.

My parents were not religious. They never went to church. But fortunately for me, my maternal grandmother, who had died long before this, was a Christian Science practitioner. Thus, my mother and father knew about healing with the mind. They decided there was nothing to lose; they hired a practitioner.

I do not remember specifically what the practitioner talked about,

but he drummed into my young mind that anything is possible and I would be healed. And I was! Completely. It did not happen overnight but over the next few months I gained weight, strength, and my heart returned to normal. The doctors were astounded. One specialist wrote a medical paper and made a presentation at the hospital on the "miracle" of my recovery. I remember this because he took me to the hospital and I sat on the podium as proof of my recovery while he gave the talk.

The impression made on my young mind was that this healing power was in my subconscious mind. Since that episode I have had a passion for finding out all I could about the subconscious mind—how it works and how to use it.

I found my genie and learned how to use it. Now I want to help you find and use your genie. The good news is that you do not have to look for it. You already have it—it is your subconscious mind. Your subconscious mind, like any benevolent genie, will grant your wishes. It will help you achieve goals, replace undesirable habits, and more. All you have to do is learn to be its master, not its puppet.

Learning to use more of your subconscious mind is easy and in this book, you will learn to:

- Change undesirable habits
- Increase self-esteem
- Learn faster and retain more
- Be successful
- Improve your memory (actually, your recall)
- Be more creative
- Improve your mental and physical health
- Communicate with your subconscious mind to verify hunches, interpret dreams, etc.
- Teach your subconscious mind to work *with* your conscious mind rather that against it
- Motivate yourself and improve work habits
- Monitor the input to your subconscious mind
- Relax more completely and sleep better
- How to instantly transform a gloomy mood into a joyous one

COURSE OUTLINE

A paradigm on how your subconscious mind works is described, and based on the way it works, ten methods are given for using your subconscious mind to achieve your goals. The paradigm and the methods are logical and simple. Do not be fooled into thinking that because the methods are easy that they are not powerful. Occham's razor, a principle taught in philosophy class, states that when many theories are available to explain a phenomenon, the simplest one is most likely the correct one. Nature seeks the simplest way.

I could give you complex methods with the simple, basic principles woven in. You would achieve the same results but it would take more time. But if they were more complex you would probably lose interest and not bother doing them. So just be grateful that these methods are easy.

Is this paradigm absolutely correct in every aspect? Probably not. Is it an over-simplification? Probably so. The brain is too complex for anyone to say they understand exactly how it works. James Watson, of the National Academy of Sciences stated that, "The human brain is the most complex thing we have uncovered in the universe." Until recently, the live brain has been difficult to study. Brain research has increased because new noninvasive tests and powerful computers are available. After reading the first part of *The Genie Within,* you will see the paradigm is logical and serves as a map that shows how to use your subconscious mind and make it your personal genie.

Lesson One lists examples demonstrating how powerful our subconscious minds are. The four states of mind and their roles are also discussed.

The basic differences between the conscious mind and subconscious mind, in layman terms, are discussed in Lesson Two.

The subconscious mind as a goal-seeking biocomputer is discussed in Lesson Three. It is essential to understand how your computer works to use it effectively.

A few subtle, but *critical*, laws of the subconscious mind are covered in Lesson Four.

The importance of communication between the conscious mind and subconscious mind is discussed in Lesson Five and five methods of communicating with your subconscious mind are described. Communicating with your subconscious mind is necessary to get your conscious mind and subconscious mind working together in harmony. It is also convenient for

deciphering dreams, verifying hunches, determining the cause of a malady, etc.

Ten easy methods for using your subconscious mind productively and efficiently are presented in Lessons Six, Seven, and Eight. A technique for going into a state of complete happiness is also presented.

The last lesson, referred to as the Sequel Lesson, shows how to use what you have learned in Lessons One through Eight to make your prayers a thousand times more powerful.

You have a genie that will grant your wishes. But your genie will not grant wishes simply by rubbing a lamp or uncorking a magical bottle. The genie is your subconscious mind and you must know how it works and how to use it before it will be your powerful servant. This book is your instruction manual.

The Genie Within is not "feel-good" stories and "have-faith" platitudes. Rather, it explains in layman terms what you need to know to use your magnificent, powerful subconscious mind.

People tend to underestimate the power in their subconscious mind because of their egos. Ego, conscious mind, thinks it knows best and can do anything better than their subconscious mind can. Yes, conscious mind is more intelligent, but it is nowhere near as powerful or capable as your genie. Allow yourself to read *The Genie Within* with an open (conscious) mind. Do not let your ego keep you from learning how to put your genie to use.

YOUR GENIE

Lesson One

YOUR GENIE

The capability of your subconscious mind is far beyond what you think it is. Many experts claim that most of us use only ten percent of our subconscious mind. After this lesson, you will see why a few pundits believe most of us use less than three percent. Before I go over a few of the feats the subconscious mind is capable of, I need to clarify a couple of definitions.

First, you need to know what I mean by conscious and subconscious minds. The part of your brain that you are aware of is your conscious mind. On the flip side, the part of your mind you are unaware of is your subconscious mind. It is that simple: everything in these lessons is simple.

Another aspect of the mind that needs clarifying is the difference between "brain" and "mind." The brain is that three-pound organ in your head. The "mind" is something larger and more elusive. There is a huge difference between brain and mind and there are books that go into intricate details on these differences. From a Western point of view, the *brain* is the physical anatomy and the mind is what the brain generates through its activity. From an Eastern point of view, some say, the mind is the source of the thoughts supplied to the brain. For the purpose of this course the difference is not important so the words, "brain" and "mind," are used interchangeably.

Recent discoveries in the new field of psychoneuroimmunology show that the brain is not confined within the cranium—it actually extends throughout the body.

Mind and body are no longer two distinct entities. Your mind can control, directly or indirectly, the body and vice versa. This new field is exciting but, again, for our purposes, you can think of the brain simply as that wrinkled organ in your head.

Just a few decades ago our medical establishment said it was impossible to control involuntary functions, such as heart rate, body temperature, and blood pressure. They were partially right. It is impossible to *directly* control involuntary functions. But involuntary functions can be controlled indirectly by using the conscious mind to communicate your intent to the subconscious mind.

Biofeedback is now an accredited method in the medical profession for controlling involuntary functions. A few of its capabilities are reducing blood pressure, stress, anxiety, and eliminating migraine headaches. But a doctor's prescription, an expensive, sophisticated instrument, and a skilled technician are required.

Biofeedback is not the only way to influence your subconscious mind. There are other ways that are easy and cost nothing. The purpose of this book is to explain these ways in easy-to-follow steps.

DIFFERENT, *REALLY* DIFFERENT

The crux of using your subconscious mind is to appreciate how different it is from your conscious mind. Even though the conscious mind and subconscious mind exist in the same body, they have vastly different characteristics. If another man or women communicated with you as your subconscious mind communicates with you in dreams, for example, you would think the man or woman was crazy. But your subconscious mind is not crazy just because your dreams are obscure to your conscious mind; it is just different.

Carrying this analogy further, consider the huge difference between men and women. Besides the physical differences, there are emotional differences and, as a result, men and women interact differently. A popular book explains these differences. Most men are goal-oriented and want to work out their problems alone. Most women are more into relationships and feelings. They need to talk to someone who just listens. These are valid differences, but even if you do not know this much, men and women can still talk and get along. At worst, if the differences are too large, they can go their separate ways.

But your conscious mind and subconscious mind cannot be separated. And, if they do not work together, the results can be harmful. Results can be, for examples poor health, seeking destructive relationships, and inappropriate behavior, such as, poor eating habits and temper outbursts.

The subconscious mind contains the software for your involuntary functions, emotions, and habits. Most of your habits and emotional conditioning were programmed in early childhood before you had mature faculties to make proper decisions. Many were programmed haphazardly and usually by parents, teachers, peers, TV and, recently, perhaps, computer games. Freud said, "We learn as children how we react emotionally and this is carried into adulthood. When we are children, we do not have the faculties that we do in adulthood. We do not know what we are going to need in adulthood to cope. Therefore, as adults we (often) react as children."

These old programs are still influencing, if not controlling, your behavior even though many are counterproductive. Some may even be destructive. When you understand the subconscious mind and a few laws it obeys, you can change these childhood programs. You will become the master of your genie.

THE POWER OF
THE SUBCONSCIOUS MIND

The subconscious mind has a largely untapped potential. A few observed feats of which the subconscious mind is capable, are listed below. Examples in this section are extraordinary feats performed by human beings with ordinary minds and bodies (except for the athletes). If these ordinary people, with ordinary subconscious minds, can do these feats, then you and I can do them. But to do them, we must rely on our subconscious minds, not our conscious minds. The conscious mind cannot make your body do these feats. The conscious mind has to know how to tap the subconscious mind to do them.

The following feats were performed without drugs or prayer. In addition to the following examples, there are miraculous healings of the body, such as spontaneous remissions of cancer or other diseases attributed to prayer or a visit to a sacred place, such as Lourdes. Such cases have been documented. But the power of prayer is another subject. Prayer is addressed in a sequel lesson.

I will start with stage hypnotists. Most of you have had an opportunity to see one perform. Essentially, all they do is plant a suggestion in the subconscious mind of the subject. But the results, to our conscious minds, seem extraordinary.

■ I witnessed a hypnotist tell a man that he just returned from another planet, and he asked the subject to describe his visit to this planet. The subject

demonstrated a vivid imagination by describing the planet in detail. This person in a normal mental state would probably avow he has a poor imagination. Maybe his conscious mind has poor imagination, but his subconscious mind has a vivid one. Moreover, in a normal mental state he would, likely, not be able to vividly and spontaneously describe something in such detail from his imagination in front of a large audience.

- Hypnotic subjects can exhibit extraordinary strength. I have a picture from a national newspaper that appeared many years ago of Johnny Carson suspended between two chairs. Kreskin, the well-known mentalist (he refuses to be called a hypnotist), planted a suggestion in Carson's subconscious mind that he was super strong and that he could keep his body rigid. He had Carson place his head on one chair and the soles of his feet on another. Carson remained rigid even when someone sat on his stomach. If it was not for the fact that his subconscious mind accepted the suggestion, Carson could not have performed this feat. (Do not do this. You could strain a muscle.)

- A suggestion planted in a subject's subconscious mind can change his personality and make him or her do things they would not do under normal circumstances. I witnessed stage hypnotists make: an ordinary woman strut around the stage acting as if she had just won the Miss America contest; a man pursue a broom stick acting as if it were a gorgeous movie star, and; a man attack (he had to be held back) a larger man, who he knew was a muscled college wrestler, because the wrestler kicked an imaginary dog.

■ Hypnotized subjects can be made amnesiac. A woman volunteer on a PBS TV program was hypnotized and she was told to forget the number 7. Later, when out of the hypnotic state, they took her to a stage set up like a game show. The host told her she would win $1,000,000 for answering this simple question: What is 4 plus 3? She could not come up with the correct answer. They gave her two more chances with two more simple questions in which the answer was 7. Each time she could not recall the number 7. They then asked her to count the fingers on her hands. She counted 1,2,3,4,5,6,8,9,10,11. She could not say the number 7. She was also confused about having 11 fingers.

■ Some doctors, dentists, and therapists use hypnosis for medical purposes. I recently read, for example, that hypnosis is being used on severe burn patients. Other examples include control of chronic pain, anesthesia, birthing, and eliminating phobias. On the same PBS TV show mentioned above, a hypnotherapist cured a woman of a lifelong fear of snakes in just a few minutes. She fearlessly held a boa constrictor and let it wrap around her shoulders. The hypnotherapist also cured a man with a lifelong fear of spiders. The man let a tarantula crawl on his shoulders.

■ Dr. James Esdaile, a Scottish surgeon, practicing in the 1800's used hypnotism in operations before anesthesia was available. His rate of success was ten times above that of his colleagues. The hypnotized patients felt less pain and anxiety, which allowed their immune systems to repress infections. Dr. Esdaile also planted suggestions in their subconscious minds to expedite healing. The

mortality rate for operations in the mid 1800's was 50 percent. In 161 operations performed by Dr. Esdaile using hypnosis, the mortality rate was a mere 5 percent.

■ A young man I knew was embarrassed about the thick glasses he wore. He read two books by Margaret Darst Corbett who wrote about the theory of ophthalmologist, Dr. William H. Bates. Dr. Bates believed that poor eyesight was epidemic in our society due to stress caused by our hectic culture. This stress tensed the eye muscles, which distorted the eyeball. The distorted eyeball shifted the focal point and blurred vision. Dr. Bates cited examples of aboriginal cultures, which were free of the stresses of modern societies, where the people seldom had poor eyesight, even at old age.

Dr. Bates's cure was eye exercises designed to relax the muscles in the eye sockets so the eyeballs could return to their original shapes, making the use of glasses unnecessary. Eliminating eyeglasses was not popular with opticians, oculists, and ophthalmologists. It was not popular with anybody else either because the exercises were tedious, required dedication, and results were uncertain.

The young man used his subconscious mind (the method discussed in Lesson Eight) to relax his eye muscles. Within weeks he could read without glasses.

■ Phantom pregnancies (pseudocyesis) occur in some woman due to psychological reasons. When a woman has a phantom pregnancy, her subconscious mind causes:

• Cessation of menstruation

• Breast enlargement

- Desire for strange foods
- Progressive abdominal enlargement
- Labor pains

■ Impressive examples of the power of subconscious mind have been reported in medical journals in cases of patients with multiple personality disorder. Multiple personality disorder occurs when, due to severe psychological trauma, a person develops more than one personality to cope. Cases have been reported in which one personality:

- Has asthma while another personality—in the same body—does not have asthma. Incidentally, cases of patients in which the doctor (one case was reported by Carl Jung) found that the asthma was due to a traumatic experience associated with breathing. Thus, the subconscious mind is capable of creating asthma. So one would assume it is also capable of eliminating it.

- Has a high IQ, while another has a low IQ. This is not so impressive because it is easy for the subconscious mind to make anyone act dumb.

- Is drunk, but when the person changes personalities, is sober. This is impressive because the subconscious mind, it seems to me, has to alter the chemistry in the brain.

- Is right-handed; the other is left-handed.

- Has different colored eyes from the other personality. I knew a man who changed the color of his eyes from brown to blue. It took him weeks to do it. But the person with multiple personality disorder does it in minutes.

- Has scars, cysts, or tumors, while the other does not. This is plausible because there are records of hypnotists who have caused blisters to form on subjects and then make them disappear just as fast. The hypnotists touch the subjects with an ordinary object, such as a pencil, suggesting to them that it is a red-hot poker, and blisters form. Then the hypnotists suggest the subjects' skin is normal and the blisters disappear.

- Has an immediate healing. A multiple personality disorder patient who was allergic to wasp bites was stung near the eye. The eye area swelled so much that he was rushed to a hospital. Before arriving at the hospital, he changed personalities and the swelling disappeared.

■ This following experiment demonstrates the effect our attitudes and beliefs can have on our bodies and health. In 1985, a Harvard professor, Ellen Langer, conducted an experiment that showed people could become younger[1]. The professor recruited 100 people over 70 years old in the Boston area. She sent them on a 10-day vacation to a resort where she arranged the decor to resemble that of the 1950's, a time when the subjects were decades younger. She played 50's music, displayed 50's magazines and newspapers, and had the subjects dress as they did in the 50's. The professor also instructed the 100 people to "act as if" they were back in the 1950's.

Physical and psychological tests were performed on the 100 subjects before and after the 10 days. In every

---

[1] Langer, Ellen. *Mindfulness,* Perseus Books, 1989

category, the subjects tested younger. What changed? What took years off their apparent age? The only cause was a change in their thinking. Their subconscious minds accepted the concept of being younger.

■ Your conscious mind sets limits for you. When you rid yourself of these limits, and let your subconscious mind take over, you can do things you thought impossible. Fifty years ago, experts wrote papers explaining why the human body could not run a mile in less than four minutes. Everyone, except Roger Banister, thought that running a mile in less than four minutes was impossible. When Banister broke the four-minute barrier in 1954, other runners duplicated the feat within months. What changed in these other runners? They did not  magically become better conditioned or alter their running style. They changed their *belief!* They now knew a four-minute mile was possible, and if Roger could do it, they could do it.

■ Vasily Alexeev, a world-class Russian weightlifter, could not lift 500 pounds though he routinely lifted 495 pounds. In 1974, his coach played a trick on him to prove a point. He put 500 pounds on the bar and told Vasily the bar had 495 pounds on it. Thinking it was only 495 pounds, Vasily lifted the bar as usual. After Vasily was told he had lifted 500 pounds, he changed his belief and was able to do it in competition.

■ A trained athlete lifting 500 pounds is not as impressive as a mother in panic lifting a car that has fallen on her son. How can she do it? Because in panic her conscious mind is put aside and does not tell her it is impossible. She has an adrenalin rush and just does it. I have only heard of such stories secondhand but a similar story appeared in the *Phoenix Gazette.* An incident was reported about a mechanic who lifted a car off two friends after it slipped off a tow bar. He also helped them out from under the car while holding it on his knees.

These are but a few examples that demonstrate the power in the subconscious mind, and this power is available in *your* subconscious mind.

CAVEATS

You will get results if you follow the rules and methods outlined in these lessons. You will achieve goals efficiently and faster than you thought possible. It is more than likely that you will not credit these lessons for your successes. One reason is that nothing dramatic happens during or after programming your subconscious mind. A chorus of angels or band of trumpets does not announce that your affirmations are working or that you have achieved your goals. It just happens—it happens naturally and without conscious effort.

If you look for signs, question your progress, or interfere in any way by using your conscious mind, you will likely stymie or kill your progress. Changes are subtle and effortless. You must toss out your Puritan ethic of hard work. For if you work hard at it, that is, with your conscious mind, your conscious effort will work against you. Your subconscious mind, your genie, works unconsciously and effortlessly. The less you strain, the more you relax and let it happen, the more

successful you will be. This will make more sense after the first three lessons. So read on, relax, and enjoy success!

STATES OF MIND

Using your subconscious mind effectively requires being in an altered state of mind. This altered state is natural, but it is different from your normal awake state of mind. The first proof of the need to use an altered state to access the subconscious mind, as far as I know, was demonstrated by the work of Elmer and Alyce Green at the Menninger Foundation from 1964 to 1973. The husband-wife duo studied individuals who did what seemed, at the time, superhuman feats. They studied, among others, Indian fakirs while they were buried alive for six days, laid on a bed of nails, or changed their heart rates and body temperatures. They studied Jack Schwarz, of Oregon, while he pierced himself through the arm with unsterilized metal rods. Schwarz controlled his bleeding, never became infected, and the wounds healed rapidly without leaving a mark. The Greens measured such things as body temperature, skin resistance, blood pressure, pulse, and brain waves.

These subjects had one thing in common while they performed these extraordinary feats: *they were in altered states of mind.*

There are four states of mind, *beta, alpha, theta,* and *delta,* and they are distinguished by a change in brain waves measured by an electrocephalograph.

The *beta state* is our normal awake state and is characterized by a brain wave frequency of 14 cps (cycles per second) to 100 cps. Not only is the frequency higher than other states, it is more erratic. This is because our

awake mind is busy. We are aware of many things that are going on around us. This awareness is essential for conducting our daily business and survival. Our attention constantly drifts. We are in the beta state most of our awake hours.

The *alpha state is* characterized by a brain wave frequency of 8 to 13 cps. You naturally go into the alpha state many times each day, but usually only fleetingly. Occasionally you may hover in this state. You would recognize it as daydreaming. Perhaps at one time or another you became bored, for example, standing in a slow line. You stared but your concentration was not on the thing you were staring at. Your mind was someplace else. You were in alpha. The alpha state is referred to as the "meditative" state—a state of relaxed, focused concentration. When you are in this state, you lose track of time. You may have stared at the wall for five minutes, but you think, incorrectly, you were staring at the wall for only a few seconds.

The *theta state* (4 to 7 cps) is similar to the alpha state but deeper and characterized by sudden intuitive insights. These insights are global. A classic example of global insight is comparing the way Beethoven and Mozart composed music. Beethoven composed linearly, measure

by measure, often going back and forth changing notes. Mozart said that a composition would come to him all at once and in entirety. All he had to do was to write it down on paper. That is the epitome of global thinking.

Last is the *delta state* (3 cps and lower.) This is the sleep state in which there is no consciousness. Dreaming occurs in the alpha and theta states.

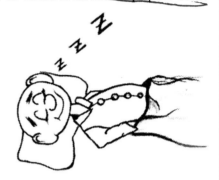

THE FOUR STATES OF THE MIND

STATE	BRAIN WAVE FREQUENCY (cycles/sec)	DESCRIPTION	COMMENTS
BETA	14 to 100	Awake	Very busy. Aware of many things.
ALPHA	8 to 13	Meditative	Focused attention. Different concept of time.
THETA	4 To 7	Inspirational	"Aha" insights. Global thoughts.
DELTA	3 and lower	Sleep	No conscious awareness.

Getting back to the Green's subjects who performed extraordinary feats, the one thing their subjects had in common when they were controlling *involuntary* body functions, was that they were in the alpha or theta states of mind. Thus, the alpha and theta brain wave states are the doorways to your subconscious mind. Your subconscious mind

will accept suggestions and commands readily when you are in the alpha and theta states of mind. Suggestions and commands to your subconscious mind are relatively ineffective when your mind is in the beta state where your conscious mind dominates.

ALPHA CONDITIONING

To use your subconscious mind effectively, you need to learn to go into the alpha state at will and stay there. Going into alpha is easy. You naturally go into it many times each day, albeit, usually only for seconds. It takes a little practice to go into the alpha or theta state at will and stay there. Exercises that teach you to go into these states are given after each lesson. The theta state is probably even more effective, but rather than referring to both the alpha and theta, I will simply refer to the alpha state from here on.

Now I am going to give you a very easy way to plant a suggestion in your subconscious mind while in the alpha state. It goes by two long names.

HYPNOPOMPIC AND HYPNAGOGIC PERIODS

These are just fancy names for the short periods when you wake in the morning and fall asleep in the evening. When you wake in the morning and when you fall asleep at night, you go from delta to beta and beta to delta states, respectively. As you do, you pass through the alpha and theta states. So twice each day you have an opportunity to program your subconscious mind while in the alpha state. This is also why you should never go to bed while worrying. Worry is a powerful affirmation and you would be implanting this powerful, negative affirmation directly into your subconscious mind.

EXERCISE

THE MENTAL ALARM CLOCK

The Mental Alarm Clock is an exercise you can do tonight. After you go to bed and as you feel yourself getting drowsy, but just before you lose control of your thoughts, say to yourself "I am wide awake at, say, 5:55 a.m. Saturday, September 25," or whatever tomorrow's date is. Use a time five minutes before your mechanical alarm clock rings. That way you will not be anxious of oversleeping. Also, use visualization. Picture your alarm clock ringing at the time you select. Exaggerate. See your alarm clock reach out and shake you awake. Some people do not use a mechanical clock because their mental alarm clock is infallible.

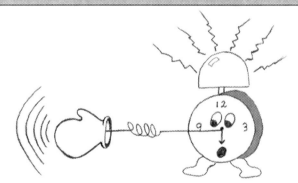

EXERCISE

GETTING INTO THE RIGHT ATTITUDE

Before we go on, you have to get into the right attitude. There is a psychological barrier you must overcome. The barrier is, "You do not get something for nothing." The price of this book is virtually "nothing" compared to what it is worth. If this book were taught as a course by a big-name guru it would cost more than $500. I paid thousands of dollars for books and courses, and I spent countless hours reading to obtain the information distilled into this course. So you need

to convince your subconscious mind that just because this book did not cost much, it is, nevertheless, extremely valuable. So, to get into the right attitude, you may either pay me $500 (Just send me a check. I trust you.), or you may do the following exercise. The choice is yours.

You have not learned about some key mental attitudes yet. After we have had a chance to go over them, the importance of this exercise will be clear. These attitudes are essential for getting the most out of these lessons. So for now, just trust me and do the following exercise. The key attitudes are DESIRE, EXPECTATION, and CONFIDENCE. When you pay $500 for a seminar led by a well-known motivator, you go into his or her classroom with a strong DESIRE to "get it", whatever "it" is. You EXPECT to get it or you would not have paid $500. Lastly, you have utmost CONFIDENCE in the teacher or again you would not have paid him or her $500.

You are going to do a little bit of acting. First, let me assure you that you are a good actor. Some psychologists would say you are always acting—acting out the role that you think others expect you to play. It is time to act. Grab your left forearm with your right hand and hold on to it. Act as if your right hand is stuck to your left arm. No matter how hard you try to pull it off, you cannot pull your right hand away from your left arm. The harder you try, the more it sticks. Go ahead and try to pull your right hand away from your left arm, but you cannot! Okay, that is enough. Now act as if your right hand is normal and take it off your left arm. See. You can act.

Now you are ready for a bigger acting role. First, get comfortable and relax. Sit in a soft chair and place your feet flat on the floor. Visualize a pleasant scene. For example, say you went on a dream vacation to Hawaii. Remember how it was. Picture yourself on the beach. Imagine that you are there now. Feel the gentle Trade Winds blowing across your body. Feel the heat of the sun on your body. Listen to the wind

passing through the palm trees. Relax as if you have not a care in the world. Let your mind wander. Just feel the joy of being at your favorite place.

Have someone else read the following to you in a quiet, slow voice. Better yet, record it and play it back. If neither option is available, or you simply do not want to take the time to record it, that is okay. Just do your best to stay in this relaxed mood and read the following to yourself. As you read it, visualize the following scene as vividly as you can. See it, feel it, and hear it.

Before you start, pretend an expert, an expert you trust, has hypnotized you. You know what hypnotized people look and act like. They look totally relaxed and if their eyes are open, they seem to stare without seeing. If someone is going to read the following to you, then shut your eyes and show complete relaxation. Your head is probably cocked to one side resting on your shoulder and your arms are hanging limply at your sides. If you are going to read the following to yourself, then act like you have been hypnotized and the hypnotist has asked you to open your eyes and read the following, but under a deep hypnotic state. Okay, go on.

> *Picture yourself on a stage. You are an actor rehearsing for an important play. Nobody else is in the auditorium except me, the author and director of the play. I am coaching you. Now in the first scene you must project the emotion of strong DESIRE. Think of a time when you felt a strong DESIRE...a time when you experienced a strong motivation to accomplish something. Maybe it was winning a game, or getting an "A" on a test. See yourself in your mind's eye. See yourself pucker up your face and set your jaw in determination. See how you acted. Relive how you felt. Hear what was going on at the time. Get absorbed in the atmosphere of this strong DESIRE.*
>
> *Now picture this book. Picture yourself reading these lessons and learning these lessons. Overlay the picture of yourself studying*

these lessons over the picture of the time you had a strong DESIRE. Let these sensations set in for a minute...

Now it is time to rehearse the next scene in the play. In this scene, you are to emote the feeling of showing a high EXPECTATION. This scene is easy. Just remember, say, a Christmas Eve or Hanukkah, when you were young. If it is a Christmas, see all the presents under the Christmas tree. Visualize the bright colored wrappings and colored bows. Remember how eager you were to open those presents...to find out what is in those packages. Recall how you could not wait. You thought you would burst from anxiety. Recall how you could not sleep that night because the EXPECTATION was so intense. See, and feel, and hear the atmosphere of that eve. Now allow these sensations to set in for a minute...

Now overlay that mental picture of a time when you felt a strong EXPECTATION with the picture of yourself reading and learning these lessons. Superimpose this picture of reading this book over the picture of Christmas Eve while experiencing the same feelings and emotions.

Now it is time to rehearse the last scene. In this scene, you must show complete CONFIDENCE, so start by showing absolute CONFIDENCE in the director and author of your play. Look out into the audience at me and emote confidence in my ability to direct you...

Now again, overlay this picture of yourself reading and studying these lessons.

Allow this feeling of CONFIDENCE to sink in.

Now it is time to awake from the hypnotic state. Picture me as the director of your play saying to you, "You are fully awake on the count of "3." I am going to count from 1 to 3 and as I do you return to a fully awake state of mind. "1," you are waking up..."2," acting like you feel refreshed and relaxed..."3" you are wide awake!

Do you think that was too easy to be of any value? I will say it again, "If it is not *easy*, if it is not *effortless*, then you are not doing it right!" So lighten up! The methods you will learn in this book are easy; if you exert effort, you will fail.

Do you believe you were hypnotized? You probably do not. But do not be too certain about that. If you were not hypnotized, you were not acting. Some experts believe that hypnosis is nothing more than acting.

To prove hypnosis is acting, on a TV show aired on PBS, a professor asked a volunteer to *act* as though he was hypnotized. The professor did nothing else. No induction. No staring at a candle flame or a swinging pendulum. The volunteer assumed the typical hypnotized look. He appeared to be completely relaxed. His head rested on his shoulder. His eyes were closed. His arms and hands hung limply at his sides. The professor then said, "Here is a delicious apple. You may eat it while I talk to the host." The object the professor handed the volunteer was not an apple—it was a Spanish onion. Nevertheless, the volunteer ate the onion thinking it was a delicious apple. This volunteer was never hypnotized by any standard routine. He was only *acting* as though he were hypnotized!

So, if you really imagined the acting scenes, you were hypnotized, or more importantly, you were in the alpha state.

An accredited hypnotist states on his web page that if you close your eyes and imagine yourself walking through your house, or apartment, opening each door as you walk through it, you were hypnotized while you were imaging it. Hypnosis can be that simple.

DIFFERENCES
Between the
Subconscious Mind
and the
Conscious Mind

Lesson Two

INTRODUCTION

Understanding your subconscious mind is essential in order to use it effectively. To begin with, you must be aware of the differences between the conscious mind, which you are familiar with, and the subconscious mind, which you are not familiar with. Below are the inherent differences in layman terms.

THE BRAIN

Most of you are familiar with the "Right-Brain, Left-Brain" Theory. Briefly, the left side of your brain (for most people) processes language capability, thinks linearly, and is logical, whereas the right side of your brain is intuitive and senses the whole, rather than parts.

Some experts believe this theory is an over-simplification. Much of the research leading to this theory, at least initially, was obtained from epileptic patients who had the left and right sides of their brains surgically disconnected for medical reasons. In normal people, there is considerable feedback between both sides and, in special cases, one side can acquire the capabilities of the other. We will not use this model in this course.

We will consider the "Triune Model" of the brain developed by Dr. Paul MacLean, Chief of the Laboratory of Brain Research and Behavior, National Institute of Mental Health. The Triune model is based on three stages of evolution, the "Reptilian," "Mammalian," and "Cortex." Each stage

represents a different type of mentality geared to the needs that prevailed at the time. Each is a separate computer with its own special intelligence, subjectivity, sense of time and space, and memory. For our purposes, it is convenient to combine the first two parts, which are by far the oldest parts (the reptilian and mammalian parts) and call it the subconscious mind.

REPTILIAN

The first stage of the brain evolved 250 million years ago and is called the "reptilian brain," or the "brain stem." It stopped changing 250 million years ago. Thus, the reptilian brain in man is essentially the same as in all reptiles. It is involuntary, impulsive, and compulsive; it contains programmed responses that are rigid. This part of the brain is paranoid for self-preservation. Paranoia is useful for keeping an eye out for enemies or, more to date, for cars when crossing the street. This part of the brain does not learn from experiences. It just tends to repeat its programmed behavior over and over.

The reptilian brain evolved for survival. It controls basic functions necessary for life, including heart rate, breathing, fighting, fleeing, feeding, and reproduction. It has no feelings.

MAMMALIAN

The mammalian brain evolved about 50 million years ago. The mammalian brain in man is also essentially the same as in all mammals. This part of the brain contains *feelings* and *emotions*. It is playful and the source of maternal care. Mammals tend to their young; reptiles usually do not.

The mammalian part of the brain provides us with feelings of what is real, true, and important to us, but it is inarticulate in communicating these feelings to the conscious mind. Important features are that the subconscious mind (1) is the source of feelings and derives information in terms of feelings, and (2) derives its value system by experience, that is, experience with emotional impact.

CORTEX

The third stage of development is the "cortex." It is the conscious part of the mind. According to Carl Jung, the famous psychiatrist, it is about 40,000 years old and is still evolving. Some contemporary researchers think it is older. An important feature of the conscious mind is that it does not begin to develop until about age three and is not fully developed until about 20 years of age. These ages vary between individuals.

This late development is one reason we have so many negative and counterproductive programs in our subconscious minds. When the emotional part of our brains was developing in the early years of our lives, we did not have a rational, mature conscious mind to filter out negative programs and select positive ones we will need as adults. To make matters worse, we are not aware of most of these programs now because they were developed at such an early age we have no conscious memory of them.

In contrast to the subconscious mind, which evolves its value system through emotions, the conscious mind evolves its value system through rational interpretation of experience.

Because of these vast differences, "...the three brains are often dissociated and in conflict."[1]

Ken Keys, author and lecturer, stated it well: "Although our cerebral cortex has more processing capacity than any computer ever built, unfortunately the new brain isn't wired into the old brain with the monitoring feedback, and control circuits that we need for optimal functioning. Thus the new brain, the conscious mind, will analyze problems and come up with rational solutions, often without the vaguest idea what is taking place in the old brain, the subconscious mind, which is governed by nonrational feeling...that is the crux of our problem. The poor communication between the old and new brains creates problems in everyday life. For example, the old brain can bypass the thinking brain's control systems and act out intense emotions that have been bottled up in the unconscious for decades...often making mountains out of molehills. The new brain, operating in present time, realizes that the person has strength, competence, and self-worth, yet the unconscious continues to trigger ineffective, inappropriate responses to life's challenges based on negative childhood programming."[2]

[1] *The Brain,* Time-Life Books
[2] Science of Mind Magazine, p. 38, May, 1996

SIZE

The subconscious mind makes up an estimated 92% of the total brain. The conscious mind comprises the remaining 8%. Thus, the conscious mind is puny compared to the subconscious mind.

SIGHT

The conscious mind sees with the eyes. It perceives outside experiences that are taken into our minds. It is your conscious mind that sees this printed page.

The subconscious mind, on the other hand, has no contact with the outside world. It is blind. The subconscious mind does not see any more than a computer sees. Consequently, the subconscious mind does not know the difference between *real* and *imagined*. This last statement is important and will be repeated again and again. It is not conjecture; psychologists have verified it in laboratory experiments.

The subconscious mind relies on sensory input. Thus, it responds to *reality* and *imagination* in the same way. For example, when you dream of a monster, your body responds the same as it would if the monster were real. The "fight or flight" mechanism jumps into action and pumps adrenalin into your blood stream. Your body responds by sweating, increased heart rate, etc. In reality, there is no monster and no real threat.

COMMUNICATION

Most thoughts in the conscious mind are communicated by an inner or outer voice. Most, although not all, thinking uses a voice, and a voice uses words. The conscious mind communicates predominantly with words. That is one reason a large vocabulary is important. Words are the tools of thinking.

The subconscious mind has limited vocabulary and is not as articulate with words. Most people do not dream in words. The subconscious mind communicates predominantly with images and feelings. For example, you (your conscious mind) might say, "I am frightened, but I do not know why," while your subconscious mind might produce a dream in which a monster chases you.

FUNCTIONS

The conscious mind controls the voluntary functions. For example, I can consciously move my arm up or down. I can walk over here or there. These are conscious actions.

A critical factor is that *the conscious mind can only do one thing at a time.* It cannot do two things simultaneously. Someone may argue that they can read and watch TV at the same time. If you really become aware of what you are doing at an instant, you will see that you are either reading *or* watching TV. To do both requires that you quickly switch back and forth.

Recall the first time you tried to pat yourself on the top of your head and, at the same time, rub your stomach in a clockwise motion. You could not do it at first; not until you very quickly shifted one function to your subconscious mind. Then it became easy. Then when you were instructed to reverse the functions, that is, to rub the top of your head and pat your stomach, it again became difficult. It may have only taken seconds to learn one function and relegate it to your subconscious mind, in which case, doing both at the same time again became easy.

A recent article in the *New York Times* reported a scientific study that showed people cannot consciously drive and talk on their cell phone at the same time. In other words, you are doing one or the other consciously, but not both simultaneously. Using magnetic resonance images of brain

activity, the scientists found the brain has a finite amount of space for tasks requiring attention. One scientist commented that when you really want to listen to someone on the phone, you close your eyes.

Another article in a newspaper reported a mother who was so rapt in a cell phone conversation she got off the bus without her four-month-old baby.

A simple experiment will prove that your conscious mind can only do one thing at a time. Pick up a light object such as a pen. Will yourself to drop it. Easy! To drop the pen you had to make a conscious decision *when* to drop it. Now hold the pen and continue saying to yourself, "I can drop it; I can drop it..." on and on. If you truly concentrate on the one thought, the thought that you can drop the pen, then you cannot make the decision *when* to drop the pen. If you cannot make the decision when to drop the pen, then you cannot drop it. You cannot continuously think, "I can drop the pen" and at the same time consciously think "Now, I will drop the pen."

Think about when you learned to drive a car. Many of us learned in a car with a stick shift. The first lesson went like this. You turned the key on. The car lurched and the engine died because we forgot to put the gear in neutral. You started the car again but it died because you did not give the engine more gas. You were thinking of turning the key. You started the car again and gave it some gas. You shifted gears only to hear a clash. You had forgotten to push in the clutch. Now you pushed down on the clutch pedal and shifted into first gear. You let off on the clutch and the engine died. You did not think to give it more gas. Finally, the car started moving and your dad screamed, "Look out!" Oops, you were not steering; you were thinking of shifting gears.

Learning to drive is a good example of how difficult it is for the conscious mind to do many things at once. However, after you relegated one function after another to the

subconscious mind, driving became easy—it no longer required conscious effort.

Hitting a golf ball is another example. When you are learning, there are too many things to think about during the swing. A beginner's swing is awkward and often jerky. After you transfer each step to your subconscious mind, you do not have to think about your swing at all. In fact, thinking about your swing (a conscious mind activity) interferes with it.

The subconscious mind, in contrast, can do trillions of functions at the same time. We do not have to conscientiously think to breathe, perspire when we are hot, digest our food, fight foreign bodies, release insulin, and on and on. This subject is discussed again in the next lesson when we explore the subconscious mind as a computer.

Your subconscious mind constantly communicates with all of the cells in your body, and the cells, in turn, communicate with your subconscious mind. To learn more of this fascinating subject read *Molecules of Emotion by* Candice Pert, a pioneer in the new medical field of psychoneuroimmunology.

COGNITIVE PROCESS

The conscious mind is logical. It has the ability to think, think abstractly, reason, criticize, analyze, judge, choose, select, discriminate, plan, invent and compose, use hindsight and foresight. It uses both deductive and inductive reasoning.

Your conscious mind, for the most part, filters the impact of input to the subconscious mind. Everything gets into the subconscious mind, but the conscious mind can influence the effect, or power, it has over the subconscious mind. As stated earlier, the conscious mind does not begin to develop until the age of three and it is not fully developed until about the age of 20. You did not have this filter during your critical, early formative years. Thus, you have a lot of garbage in your

subconscious mind that is counterproductive to your health, peace of mind, and productivity.

The subconscious mind, conversely, is not logical; it is the feeling mind. It is the source of love, hatred, anguish, fear, jealousy, sadness, anger, joy, desire, etc. When you say, "I feel..." the source of the feeling is the subconscious mind. Think of an extreme example, such as rage. A person expressing deep rage exhibits strong emotion, superior strength, is highly illogical, and has poor (conscious) recollection of his or her carrying on afterward.

The subconscious mind reasons inductively, from the specific to the general. If you tell it you are clumsy, it will find a way for you to do something clumsy. Usually inductive rationale is not logical.

The conscious mind thinks of words objectively. Objectively the word "mother" means a female parent. The subconscious mind, on the other hand, is subjective and adds connotations to words. When you hear the word "mother," all kinds of feelings are aroused. These feelings come from the subconscious mind.

WILL, POWER, AND WILLPOWER

The conscious mind has a sense of awareness. It knows persons, places, conditions, and things. The conscious mind knows that it knows. It contains knowledge that we are ourselves and we are here.

Importantly the conscious mind has *will*. Will is the ability of the conscious mind to initiate and direct a thought or action. Will supplies the direction of your thinking. Human beings have free will.

Ah! But the subconscious mind has the power! An article in *Psychology Today*, August 1974, stated that, "...we discovered the brain is a source of electrical energy; it can do electrical

work." Your brain produces about 25 watts of power. The subconscious mind transmits this energy as urges, emotions, impulses, nervous twitches, etc.

This energy in the subconscious mind is inexhaustible; your brain functions 24-hours-a-day, all of your life.

The wonderful thing about using the subconscious mind is that it is *effortless*. No conscious effort is required to use your subconscious mind. Conscious effort, no matter how well intended, only impedes the subconscious mind.

Doing something with the conscious mind requires effort. Remember how learning something for the first time took effort? For example, it took a while to learn to tie a shoestring. It is complicated the first time or two. Imagine if you had to write out all the steps clearly enough so that someone who had never seen a bow could tie one.

Once tying a bow became habit—in other words, the task was relegated to the subconscious mind—it became easy. So easy, you do not have to think about it when you are doing it. In fact, you probably do not even remember tying the laces in your shoes because you did it subconsciously.

A high-jumper interviewed on TV after he set a track record said, "I do not remember my record jump, but I knew when I started to jump that I would be successful." He did not remember because he was jumping unconsciously. He let his subconscious mind take over. The subconscious mind can do all the operations without mental effort. Had he jumped using his conscious mind, it would have been an effort and he would not have done nearly as well.

The best book on this subject is *The Inner Game of Tennis* by Timothy Gallwey. Do not be turned off by the title if you are not a tennis player; just mentally cross out "tennis" as you read and insert any other word you want. Gallwey articulately describes how the conscious mind cannot do a task as difficult as hitting a tennis ball (or driving a car or

hitting a golf ball) well. Whereas, the subconscious mind can do a difficult task, and do it effortlessly and perfectly *when not interfered with by the conscious mind.* That is the trick— keeping the conscious mind out of the way. ✶

So, the conscious mind has the *will* and the subconscious mind has the *power*. When the conscious mind and subconscious mind are in harmony, you have *willpower*. You are "single-minded."

But when the conscious mind and subconscious mind are in conflict, there is no *willpower*. You are "double-minded." Your conscious mind cannot directly overpower your subconscious mind and "will" it to do something.

Emile Coué[3] (1857–1926) was highly successful in Europe in curing a variety of ills. He believed in gabbling (talking quickly and indistinctly so the conscious mind would get bored and not pay attention) an affirmation until it sank into the subconscious mind and became completely accepted by it. You've probably heard one of his familiar affirmations, "Every day, better and better in every way."

Coué said, "When *will* and *imagination* are in conflict, imagination always wins." That is to say, when the *conscious mind* and the *subconscious mind* are in conflict, the *subconscious mind* always wins. The subconscious mind wins because it has the power (it has electrical and chemical power), and it is bigger. ✶

When an overweight man wills himself to go on a diet, and if he does not change his subconscious desire for overeating, eventually his subconscious mind will win out. He will gain back any weight he lost. He may *will* himself not to eat that delicious dessert, but the urge from the subconscious mind will win. He will eat the dessert and he will eat it *effortlessly*.

[3] Information on Emile Coué can be found on the Internet and in the book by Brooks, listed in Appendix A.

Your task is to learn how the subconscious mind works and use it to your advantage. The subconscious mind has the power to dominate, but it is not as smart as your conscious mind. You are going to learn how to make it your personal genie, not your master.

MEMORY

The conscious mind has a limited memory and most of it is short-term. The subconscious mind, in stark contrast, has virtually infinite memory. You are probably thinking it does not seem that way to you. Well, it is true. You have enough memory for everything you have experienced in your life. It is your *recall* that is fallible.

CONTROL

When your conscious mind and your subconscious mind are in conflict, your subconscious mind wins, but only if you do not know how to control it. You are going to learn how to influence and control your subconscious mind so it does not control you. You are going to make it your genie! Your conscious mind is meant to be the master, and your subconscious mind is meant to be the genie.

The conscious mind can stimulate the subconscious mind into action, change habits, reverse negative thinking patterns, improve our physical and emotional health, and our conscious mind can even influence our involuntary functions.

A few decades ago, thinking in the Western world was that control of involuntary functions was impossible. The Western world now knows that controlling involuntary functions such as blood pressure, heart rate, and circulation in a given area of our bodies, is possible.

The following chart sums up the differences between conscious mind and subconscious mind:

COMPARISON OF THE CONSCIOUS MIND
AND THE SUBCONSCIOUS MIND

CHARACTERISTIC	CONSCIOUS MIND	SUBCONSCIOUS MIND
AGE	New	Old
SIZE	Small	Large
SIGHT	Sees	Blind
COMMUNICATION	Words	Images, Feelings
COGNITIVE PROCESS	Logical	Illogical
MATURITY	Mature	Immature
TIME	Past, Present, Future	Present
WILLPOWER	Will	Power
FUNCTIONS	Voluntary	Involuntary
FUNCTIONS AT ONE TIME	One	Trillions
MEMORY	Limited	Unlimited
CONTROL	**Master of the Subconscious Mind**	Body and Behavior *Your Genie*

ALPHA CONDITIONING

Your mind can be led into the alpha state by sitting in a comfortable chair and listening to a relaxation routine read by someone else, or recorded and played back. The routine usually takes about ten minutes.

You will want to go into the alpha state many times each day to give your genie instructions. It would not be practical to depend on someone else to read the routine, or to play a CD every time you wanted to go into alpha. You need to condition yourself to simply take a deep breath, count down from three to one, say to yourself the word "ALPHA," and be in alpha. It is that quick and that simple—after you are conditioned.

Conditioning exercises are given at the end of each lesson.

Alpha conditioning is easy. It just takes a little practice. Some people can condition themselves in a few sessions; others take a little longer. Closing your eyes and relaxing tends to induce alpha. Relaxation is often associated with heaviness and warmth. Once in alpha, you can condition yourself to return to this state quickly any time you want.

SELF, DEEP RELAXATION

The conditioning exercises presented in these lessons are similar to procedures called by different names. The most common is self-hypnosis. I would like to call it something else because the word "hypnosis" has negative connotations. Hypnosis is often associated with mind control or being make a fool of in front of an audience. That is unfortunate. First of all, nobody really knows what hypnotism is. Kreskin, a well-known "mentalist" (he refused to be called a hypnotist), offered $100,000 to anyone who could prove conclusively the existence of a "hypnotic trance." Nobody ever claimed the money. Kreskin never puts anyone in a trance yet he is highly successful in planting suggestions in subconscious minds.

Ernest Rossi states in *The Psychobiology of Mind-Body Healing, 1993:* "Since the inception of hypnosis more than 200 years ago it has been impossible to find general agreement among professionals on just exactly what hypnosis is. No definition or empirical test has ever been devised to accurately assess whether or not a hypnotic state even exists!" Some experts claim there is no such thing as a hypnotic trance or hypnotic state.

So let's not be concerned about what this method is called. "Self-Alphamation" (I just made up that word) would be a good descriptive word but no one would know what I was talking about. These exercises are *simply ways of going into*

the alpha state so you can plant suggestions in your subconscious mind.

An added benefit when you practice deep relaxation is that you will sleep better. Better sleep has been shown to improve health, memory, and disposition. Many people who practice deep relaxation find they need less sleep.

PROCEDURE

There is nothing magic about the routine. The routine can be done in infinite ways. You can start, for example, by relaxing muscles from the feet to head or vise versa. Any procedure that gets you to relax is good. The aim is to relax so that your conscious mind loses interest, gives up control, and sinks into the background, and at the same time, to coax your subconscious mind to the surface. Once you are in alpha, you can then use your subconscious mind to relax your body even more than you ever could when in beta using your conscious mind.

You can have someone read the routine to you or you can record it and play it back. A CD containing this routine is also available.[4]

Some self-help books describe tests to determine whether you are truly in an altered state. *Do not test yourself.* Do not doubt that you are in alpha. Should you fail the test for *any* reason, even just one time, this failure could destroy your confidence. Just act as if you know you are going to succeed and you will. Have the right attitude. Expect to relax and go into the alpha state. Be confident.

Just let go. Do not use any conscious mind activities, namely, critiquing the words, judging whether you are going

[4] A CD that includes this routine can be purchas~ WWW.THEGENIEWITHIN.NET. For more information, THEGENIEWITHIN@ROADRUNNER.COM or write to *The Genie Within,* Street, Fallbrook, CA 92028.

into alpha, etc. Use subconscious mind activities, namely visualization, daydreaming, and staying in the present. Do not think about something that happened yesterday or even ten minutes ago. Do not think about something that may happen ten minutes from now. Keep your mind in the *now*.

Audio aids are available to assist your subconscious mind into alpha. The best, in my opinion, is simply a metronome sound at 10 cps (mid alpha) or 5 cps (mid theta). This method is used by Silva International, El Paso, TX, in courses taught worldwide. Some music and sound recordings are helpful, examples include selected Mozart works,[5] and primal sounds produced by Jeffrey Thompson.[6]

Important statements that will be given to you near the end of the routine are listed below. You should know what you are being conditioned to.

- Distractions only tend to make me go deeper into alpha.
- Each time I practice going into alpha I go deeper and deeper.
- Each time I practice, I go into alpha faster and faster.
- Each time I practice, it is easier and easier.
- My subconscious mind accepts only positive, healthful suggestions.
- Each time you touch your thumb and forefinger together you are reminded to relax and remain poised.

There is also a suggestion that any time you say or think the phrase "3...2...1...ALPHA," you will return to the alpha state. After enough practice, you will not need to go through

---

[5] *The Mozart Effect* CDs, selections by Don Campbell, author of *The Mozert Effect*.
[6] *The Egg of Time* and *Child of Dream* CDs, California Institute for Human Science.

the ten-minute relaxation routine to go into alpha. You will simply say to yourself, "3...2...1...ALPHA" and you will be there.

The intent of this exercise is to go into alpha and remain aware. This is useful, for examples at times when you want to be creative, compete in sports, study for an exam, take an exam, etc. Record the following routine and play it while sitting in a comfortable chair *(see footnote on page 47)*.

ALPHA STATE ROUTINE— PROGRESSIVE RELAXATION

Look up at about an angle of 20 degrees and stare at a spot. Raising your eyes helps attain the alpha state. Now close your eyes and listen to my voice.

Right now, you desire to experience the feeling of deep relaxation...You desire to be more relaxed than you have ever been before. Deep relaxation is healthy...it allows your body to nourish and heal itself...deep relaxation allows your mind to refresh itself.

You are breathing deeply and slowly...ever so slowly.

Relaxation is easy...all you have to do is to just let go...just let go...just let your body go limp...let your muscles relax.

With deep relaxation comes the feeling of heaviness and warmth...friendly warmth...and calmness...and pleasantness. You are feeling heavier now. You are letting go...letting go.

Visualize a ball of warm, white light. Just seeing it gives you a warm, pleasant feeling. Visualize this ball of white light entering your body at your feet. As this light enters your body, your toes become heavier...Feel each toe in turn relax...sense a warmth penetrating into your feet. Now allow your feet to relax. Feel them pressing on the floor. Now this ball of light and this feeling of heaviness and warmth moves up across you ankles...and your calves...and your thighs. Your legs are now relaxed.

This peaceful ball of light and this wave of relaxation now moves into your hips. The heaviness feeling is pleasant...and feels gooood. Deep, deep healthful relaxation. Just let go...let go...let your body relax. Let you body and mind attain a healthy, natural state.

Now this ball of warm friendly light enters your torso, and you feel deep, penetrating relaxation creep up your back. Your back muscles are now relaxed...sooo relaxed. Feel them relax and become heavy. Feel your shoulders slump as they become heavier and heavier. Now, relax the muscles of your stomach and chest. And as you do, feel your torso increase in weight...pulling you down under the push of gravity. Your body is now completely relaxed. It feels wonderful...just let go...let go completely. All of your internal muscles are relaxed.

Now visualize this ball of warm heavy light flowing into your head and arms. Relax your neck muscles. Feel your neck become heavier and more relaxed. Maintain just enough muscle tone to keep your neck in a comfortable position. Feel this relaxation move down through your arms and into your fingers...all the way to your fingertips. Your arms are completely relaxed...your fingers are completely relaxed now. They are limp...Your fingers are limp and heavy.

Now you allow this feeling of relaxation to spread up through your jaw. Feel your jaw muscles relax. Feel your throat and tongue relax and all internal dialog quiets. And lastly, feel your scalp relax.

You are completely relaxed now...every muscle...every cell in your body is relaxed. You feel comfortable...you feel contented. This is such a pleasant state...soooo pleasant...soooo relaxing...soooo comfortable. Your entire body relishes this feeling...you relish this state of deep relaxation in the alpha state.

With each breath, you are more and more relaxed. With each breath, you feel better, more at ease and happier. Now visualize a pleasant scene...see yourself on the beach of a beautiful tropical island. Feel the warmth of the sun on your body. Feel the warmth of the sand on your bare feet. Feel the warm sand oozing between your toes as you press your feet into the soft, forgiving sand. See yourself sitting in a soft, luxurious lounge chair...you feel completely comfortable...completely at rest. Gaze out at the ocean. The water is calm and serene. There are gentle ocean swells that are in rhythm with your breathing...a slow, relaxing rhythm. As you breathe out, let go of tiny bits of tension that lingered in your

body. Each time you exhale, a little more tension melts and flows out of your body. Each time you exhale...you are more and more relaxed.

Smell the fresh salt air...feel the soft touch of the warm tropical breeze. In the distance you hear sea gulls...you can see the sea gulls swooping up and down near the shoreline. You hear the whisper of the breeze passing through the fronds of the palm trees lining the beach. Watch the thin palm trees sway gently in the tropical breeze.

Scoop up a fistful of sand and let it fall back on the beach. See how effortlessly it falls and forms a pile. The pile of sand is with total absence of resistance...there is a complete lack of tension.

Your eyes feast on the vivid blues and greens of the warm, clear water in the shallows of the coral reefs. You are soooo relaxed...every muscle in your body is limp...every part of your body feels heavy and relaxed...You feel a nice warm glow throughout your body that is the result of perfect, unhindered circulation...brought about by perfect relaxation. Wallow in this feeling..relish this state of mind. Know it is a healthy state...and that your body is rejuvenating itself...energizing itself...healing itself...easily and effortlessly.

Each time you relax...each time you go to this state which is your sanctuary...relaxation is easier and easier. Each time you practice deep relaxation, you relax faster and to a deeper healthy mental state...each time the feelings are deeper and more enjoyable. Each time you practice deep relaxation you reach a place where you are poised, happy, and feel healthier.

Noises or other distractions only act as signals to relax you more. Every time you hear a noise, you go deeper into your sanctuary and become ever more relaxed. All tension is melted away. You are completely relaxed...serene...happy...content.

In any emergency, you are alert and active. Your subconscious mind instantly recognizes an emergency and immediately brings you to an alert state.

You are in a natural, healthy, alpha state of mind...open to healthy, positive suggestions. Your mind only accepts suggestions

that are positive, for your and everyone else's highest good.

You return to this relaxed feeling...to your sanctuary every time you think of the word "ALPHA," with the intention of returning to this serene state of body and mind. The word alpha in ordinary conversation is just another word and is unrelated to this effect. The word "ALPHA" is effective only when you have the intent to completely relax your body and mind as it is now and enter this natural state of mind.

Any time you wish to melt the tension from your body...any time and anywhere you wish to become more serene and calm, simply touch your thumb and forefinger together. Any time you want to be relaxed, touch your thumb and forefinger together. You associate this with the feeling of calmness...serenity..relaxation...happiness...poise...and just feeling good. Touching your thumb and forefinger together relaxes you. Any time and anywhere during the day you wish to relax...any time you wish to rid your body of tension, simply touch your thumb and forefinger together. Touching your fingers together is a signal that restores you to a state of complete poise.

Now feeling wonderful...feeling relaxed...feeling healthy and whole...feeling rejuvenated...feeling rested and happy, begin to return to full wakefulness. On the count of "3" you are in the awake state and your eyes are open. "1"..."2"...feeling rested and joyful, "3"...you are awake and alert!

YOUR SUPER BIOCOMPUTER

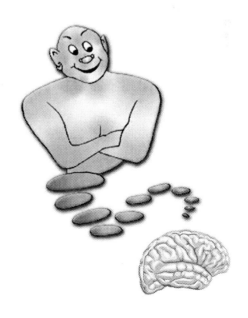

Lesson Three

YOUR SUPER BIOCOMPUTER

INTRODUCTION

While the present generation takes the personal computer for granted, its capabilities astound those of us who did not grow up with one. We are amazed at its lightning fast operation, its huge memory, and its ability to use many complex programs at the same time. As impressive as a personal computer is, your subconscious mind is a far better one than any you can buy.

Stephen Hawking, in *The Universe in a Nutshell*, says, "Present computers remain outstripped in computational power by the brain of a humble earthworm." Your brain is millions of times better than the brain of an earthworm.

It has more memory than you can ever use and operates flawlessly, except sometimes when your conscious mind interferes with it. It is easily programmed, intentionally and unintentionally. It is, unlike any manufactured computer, both electrically and chemically powered. Information travels along

nerves by electrical impulses and jumps across synapses by chemical mechanisms. Your subconscious mind is a biocomputer. Your biocomputer has been loaded with a huge number of complex programs. Most are necessary for surviving and getting along in the world. We take thousands of these programs for granted, such as walking, running, standing still, and drinking a glass of water. On the other hand, many of our programs are obsolete and counterproductive, such as impatience, over-eating, and irritability. We will now explore the facets of your personal subconscious mind biocomputer.

DATA STORAGE

Memory in your conscious mind is short-term and limited. Tests show that most people cannot remember more than seven digits at one time.

Conversely, the memory in your subconscious mind is virtually unlimited. A comedian quipped, "Memory is the thing you forget with." That is clever but not true. Every sight, sound, touch, smell, and emotion that you have experienced from birth (probably even before birth) to the present is in your memory. If you cannot remember some fact, do not blame your memory because that fact is there. Blame your *recall.*

Your brain has more storage capacity than you could ever use. Each memory creates a pathway in your brain. The narrator on a documentary on the brain aired on PBS TV stated that your brain has more pathways for memory than there are atoms in the universe! If you counted and wrote the number for each pathway in your brain on a single atom, there would not be enough atoms in the universe!

If you accept 10 new facts every second for a lifetime of 70 years, you will accept about 22×10^9 bits of information. Yet your memory capacity is about 22×10^{30} bits of information. Someone once estimated that the world's entire telephone

network could be stored in an area of your brain the size of a pea.

In 1950, Wilder Penfield, M.D. described patients undergoing brain surgery without anesthesia. When certain parts of their brains were touched with an electric probe the patients recalled everything, every sight, smell, texture and taste about a particular event in their life.

A few examples of the capability of our memory are given below:

- William James, when he was 90, memorized 12 volumes of John Milton's *Paradise Lost* in one month because he thought his memory was declining.

- Napoleon could greet 1,000's of his soldiers by their first names.

- James Farley, a politician in the Roosevelt era, could greet 50,000 people by name.

- Arturo Toscanini could recall every note of every instrument for 100 operas and 250 symphonies.

- A contemporary Indian man (I saw him interviewed on TV but I did not pay attention to his name) can recall every number he has ever seen or heard.

OPERATES CONSTANTLY

Your subconscious mind is awake 24-hours-a-day; it never sleeps. It is awake even when you are under anesthesia. Dr. Cheek, a San Francisco surgeon, reported several cases in Life Magazine ca. 1970, where he proved that patients heard conversations of the doctors during surgery.

Dr. Cheek's son was a victim of one of these conversations. His son had a congenital heart condition that was repaired. The operation was a success but his son became a hypochondriac and short-winded. By using hypnosis on his

son, Dr. Cheek found that during the operation one of the surgeons said, "...we can't fix that." On quizzing the surgeons, one said they found a second congenital defect. However, it was not serious, it was not worth the risk it would take to repair it, and since it would heal normally, they decided not to fix it. But his son's subconscious mind interpreted from the surgeons conversation that, "...we can't fix that," and erroneously concluded that his heart had a serious defect that could not be repaired. The boy's subconscious mind reacted based on its belief.

This literal acceptance by the subconscious mind brings us to the next characteristic of your subconscious mind computer. Your subconscious mind accepts things literally and out of context.

LITERAL

Your subconscious mind does not reason or judge. It takes everything literally, out of context, and with no sense of humor. If someone under hypnosis is asked, "Can you tell me your age?" The logical conscious mind would know that the hypnotist really was asking for his age, but the literal subconscious mind would simply answer, "Yes, I can."

Consider the following repetitive comments made by parents and teachers. Though they may have been made in a loving way, the subconscious mind takes them literally. And note that the conscious mind that can filter these comments is not totally effective at early ages.

- "You silly kid," or "You're so silly."
- "You big, bad boy."
- "You dummy."
- "Don't you ever learn?"

- "You never seem to do it right"
- "You must eat lots of food to be healthy."

A phenomenon called "organ language" is an example of the subconscious mind accepting words literally. Organ language refers to a dis-ease resulting from a strong emotion that gets locked in an area of your body. Alice Steadman discusses this phenomenon in her book, *Who's the Matter with Me,* and scientific support can be found in studies reported in the new field of psychoneuroimmunology.

Examples of organ language are:

- "That gives me a pain in the neck."
- "Oh, my aching back."
- "That just makes me sick."
- "That breaks my back."
- "I can't stand that."

Normally these statements have no effect on a person; but they can have a pronounced effect when they are repeated over and over or stated with strong emotion.

Lecron reports[1] a case in which a patient had a bad taste in his mouth and was losing so much weight it was affecting his health. Physicians could not find a reason for the bad taste. During analysis, Lecron found that the man was almost called as a witness in a trial. Had he testified in the trial, the defendant, his best customer, would have been found guilty. He did not have to testify but the episode left a "bad taste in his mouth."

Carl Jung reported a case in which an asthmatic patient, "Could not breathe the atmosphere at home," and a patient with chronic indigestion, "Could not digest a certain situation." Dr. Bernie Siegel reported a case[2] about a mastectomy patient

---

[1] *Self-Hypnotism: The Technique and Its Use in Daily Living*
[2] *Peace, Love & Healing*

who needed to "get something off her chest" after a long bitter dispute with her sister.

Sylvia Browne, in one of her best-selling books[3], describes a man dying of bleeding ulcers who kept repeating, "I just can't stomach life anymore." Sylvia Browne also tells a story about herself. She had a bladder infection at a time when her family, "Just pissed her off."

ACCEPTS EVERYTHING
AS REAL AND TRUE

Clinical and experimental psychologists have proved the human nervous system cannot tell the difference between an actual experience and one that is vividly imagined. Drs. J.C. Eccles and Sir Charles Sherrington, experts in brain physiology, state: "When you learn anything, a pattern of neurons forming a chain is set up in your brain tissue. This chain, or electrical pattern, is your brain's method of remembering. So, since the subconscious mind cannot distinguish a real from imagined experience, perfect mental practice can change and correct imperfect electrical patterns grooved there by habitually poor playing."

This means that you can learn and improve physical and mental skills by practicing in your mind. The advantage of using imagination is you never practice the wrong motion or action, i.e., neurological pattern. Real practice, conversely, is not perfect and often reinforces wrong neurological patterns.

Experiments have been reported in which three groups of novices are taught a new skill by three different methods. In one experiment subjects were taught dart throwing, a skill not many Americans have acquired. One group listened to lessons on the art of dart throwing. A second group threw

---

[3] *Psychic's Guide to the Other Side*

darts. The third group practiced using only imagination. This third group sat in comfortable chairs, was read a relaxation routine, and then practiced perfect dart throwing in their minds, hitting the bull's eye on each throw. After each of the three groups practiced for the same length of time, the group using mental practice always did as well, or better, than the other two.

Russian scientists did a more precise experiment. Four groups of Russian athletes trained using selected ratios of physical and mental practice as follows:

GROUP	% PHYSICAL TRAINING	% VISUALIZATION
1	100	0
2	75	25
3	50	50
4	25	75

After a given period of training, Group No. 1 ranked 4th, Group No.2, 3rd, Group No. 3, 2nd, and Group No. 4 came out on top.

Visualization is now standard in athletic training. Of course, physical practice is also necessary. Athletes use both mental and physical practice to obtain the best result. More stories of the importance of mental practice can be found in *The Ultimate Athlete,* by George Leonard.

The use of visualization is not limited to sports. It is also used successfully in job interviews, sales, public speaking, etc. See yourself giving a successful job interview; see yourself getting the job. See yourself giving a speech to a thousand happy people; feel at ease while giving the speech; hear the audience clapping and standing at the end of your speech.

YOUR BIOCOMPUTER OPERATES THE MOST PHENOMENAL ROBOT EVER MADE—YOUR BODY

Whereas your conscious mind can only do one thing at a time, your subconscious mind can do trillions of things at a time. Think of what it would take to make a computer that would control a robot that did all the things your body does. A manufactured computer could not come close to doing all the tasks your subconscious mind does every second of your life. It regulates most of the processes going on in your body every second and influences all of them in one way or another. Just a few examples of these processes include: digestion, healing, bone mending, immunity, temperature control, heart rate, respiration, reproduction (no computer can make a baby), and muscle coordination. On top of all that, it communicates with every cell in your body.

The body functions mentioned above are only a minuscule of the whole. Witness the volumes written on biology and medicine.

It is important to note that your subconscious mind does these trillions of functions without effort. It does them *easily, passively, and effortlessly*.

SOFTWARE

The software programs, often called "tapes," in your subconscious mind computer include your habits, concepts, self-images, and conditioned reflexes. We all react according to our programs when someone or some stimulus pushes our buttons.

Habits are a way of executing complicated processes easily, automatically and with no conscious mind thought. They can be useful, for example:

- Tying a bow,
- Driving a car,
- Swinging a golf club,
- Etc.

They can also be harmful, such as:

- Smoking,
- Crude manners,
- Over eating,
- Tantrums,
- Impatience,
- Etc.

Most of these habits were programmed at an early age and you are not aware of them.

When you were born, most of your existing software was in your reptilian brain. You were born with programs that controlled heart rate, body temperature, respiration, sucking, and the other basic functions necessary to keep you alive. The rest of your brain was mostly blank. Thus, your brain was like a new computer with only the basic language that allows you to install all those programs that make a personal computer useful.

Early programming of the brain was described in an article[4] summarizing current research and thinking by experts. Following is a summary of that article.

A child's brain begins as just a jumble of neurons. Every input from the five senses begins to form programs. Programs in your subconscious mind evolve progressively. For example, you learn to roll over; then you learn to crawl, walk, run, lift a glass of milk and drink it without spilling, etc. Each of these

---

[4] "Your Child's Brain," by Sharon Begley, *Newsweek,* pages 55–6, February, 1996.

activities is a huge computer program in itself. Even just standing up straight requires a complex program.

The gravity of establishing these programs is that there is a "time window." After the window closes, programming limits are set up that are difficult to overcome. Experts claim that about half of a baby's brain cells die by age five because they are not used. There are several basic time windows of development, namely; math and logic, vision, vocabulary, language, social skills, and motor skills.

The window for math and logic is from birth to four years. Even learning a simple concept like "one" versus "many," helps widen this invisible programming potential.

The window for vision is from birth to two years. This concept was demonstrated in 1970 when experimenters sewed shut one eye of newborn kittens. When the sewn-shut eyes were opened after only two weeks, the eye was blind and sight was never developed because the designated neurons were used for something else.

In another experiment, researchers raised three groups of kittens: one group in a room with only horizontal stripes, one in a room with only vertical stripes, and one in a normal room. Once removed from these rooms, the kittens raised in the room with horizontal stripes could only perceive horizontal objects. That is, they would walk into a table leg, for example, because they did not see it. The group raised in the room with vertical stripes could not perceive horizontal objects. They would not walk into a table leg, but they would walk into the table, if it were low enough, because they could not perceive the horizontal object. The third group raised in a normal room was normal.

The window of development for vocabulary is to three years. Even if a baby hears words he does not understand, on hearing these new words, neuron pathways are formed that widen the potential for learning later.

The window for language is from birth to 10 years old. Note how quickly children learn a new language compared with adults. Moreover, unless the children learn the new language at a very early age, they will most likely have an accent in that language for life.

Arguably, <u>the most important window is the emotional window, which is from birth to only two years old</u>. Think about that. Your emotional quotient is pretty much wired in the first two years of life.

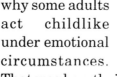

This explains why some adults act childlike under emotional circumstances.

That was how their subconscious mind was wired during the emotion window.

The window <u>for motor development is to five years old</u>. Researchers performed a landmark experiment in which a newborn monkey's hand was bound so that he could only use one finger. After the learning window passed, the binding was removed from the monkey's hand and he never learned to use his other fingers. The brain cells committed to the useless fingers were used for something else during the window of motor development.

A modern example of motor development is Andre Agassi, who has been, off and on, the number one tennis player in the world. Andre is able to change the game's strategy due to his lightening quick reflexes and ability to hit the ball early and on the rise. This takes exceptional reflexes and hand/eye coordination. Andre is also reputed to be the best ever at returning serves.

Andre's programming began when he was a few weeks old. His father dangled a ball on a string over Andre's head, and when Andre was old enough to hold something his father gave him a paddle to swing. Andre's father laid the foundation for creating a large potential for motor development in Andre's subconscious mind.

This concept of learning-windows shows the importance of exposing children to a variety of toys, colors, sounds, conversations, sights, and experiences. Of course, these programming limits are not absolute, but overcoming them can be difficult. More recent research indicates that these windows may last longer, and that the way our brains are wired in the teen years also determine how we behave as adults.

Thus, as adults, we most likely have many negative programs and concepts in our subconscious minds that were developed prior to our twentieth birthday, and many that were planted by others, namely parents, relatives, teachers, peers, TV, society, and possibly some violent video games. Unfortunately, many of these programs and concepts are counterproductive. Consider the following ones:

- Smoking,
- Overeating,
- Poor health,
- Poor self-image,
- Girls are poor in math,
- Everybody catches colds,
- "No, you cannot do that," or, "You'll never be able to do that."

Remember. The subconscious mind accepts everything as true and literal. Often well-meaning parents, repeatedly say to their children:

- "You will be a *big* girl,"
- "You are so silly,"
- "No, you can't do that,"
- "You naughty boy,"
- "You're a girl; you're not supposed to be good in math."

Some thoughtless parents or teachers might program young malleable subconscious minds with:

- "You'll never amount to anything,"
- "You will never be successful,"
- "Don't you ever learn?"
- "You are a bad boy (or girl)."
- "You will never graduate."

These negative statements will have no effect when they are said to the child only a few times. But if they are repeated, especially under emotional circumstances, they are likely to be accepted by the subconscious mind. One researcher estimated that a child is told "No" 148,000 times in his early years. No wonder the potential of so many children is unnecessarily limited.

CONDITIONED REFLEXES

Sometimes we react in irrational ways and we have no clue why. This is often due to a conditioned reflex that we are not aware of. You remember the classic experiment performed by Pavlov. When Pavlov showed a hungry dog food, the dog salivated. Pavlov then rang a bell when he showed the food to the

dog. After a few times, the dog was conditioned to the bell. Then Pavlov had only to ring the bell and the dog salivated. Ringing a bell and salivation are not ordinarily linked.

Here are a few examples of reported cases involving conditioned reflexes:

■ An adult woman abhorred spinach. Under hypnosis, she recalled a time when she was one year old. She was in a high chair eating spinach. The doorbell rang. Their German Shepard started barking and on his way to the door knocked over the high chair. Thinking her child was hurt, the mother cried and yelled. There was chaos, noise, a bump on the head, and the experience was very emotional. This traumatic experience conditioned her to dislike the food she happened to be eating when the unpleasant incident occurred. Do you suppose a similar incident happened to a previous president who dislikes broccoli and does not know why?

■ Another patient was afraid of the ocean. It turned out that, at an early age, he was on the beach when lifeguards brought in a shark-bite victim. The lurid sight was so emotional that he was conditioned to be afraid of the ocean.

■ This example was reported in *Psychotherapy,* Aug. 1974. A youngster was spanked at the end of an argument between his parents. His emotions were associated with his struggle to control the sobbing in his chest (sic). During the next argument, even without the spanking, his chest remembered.

Emotions were cut off at the chest, and the youngster developed asthma.

Each of us has thousands of programs in our subconscious minds. Most of them are useful and even essential. But many are counterproductive to a happy life. You will learn how to overcome these counterproductive programs in later lessons.

INDUCTIVE PROCESSING: GOAL SEEKING

Your subconscious computer takes thoughts from the conscious mind and works them out inductively to a conclusion. It operates from specifics to generalities. Your subconscious mind is a *GOAL-SEEKING computer*. *Your subconscious mind will act to achieve whatever goal it is given*, whether the goal is well thought out, haphazard, or provided by an outside source.

This is why monitoring what you feed your subconscious mind is important. Have you ever said to yourself, "I'm stupid"? If you said it enough and said it with emotion, your genie responded by replying, "Yes, master, I can make you look stupid. No problem. I can do it easily and effortlessly." Then, say, you took a test on a subject that you knew cold, but during the test, your mind went blank. Could it have been your subconscious mind simply obeying your command?

Ever told yourself that you are clumsy? Your genie responded by saying, "Yes, master. I can make you clumsy. That is easy and effortless." Then, for no reason, you tripped, or dropped an easy fly ball, and embarrassed yourself.

Ever say to yourself that you are shy and unpopular? If you said it often and with emotion, your genie responded, "Yes master, I can make you shy and unpopular by having you behave in unsocial ways. No problem. That is easy and effortless. You do not have to think about it. I will just do it

for you." Then after acting like a dork, you say to yourself, "Why did I act that way?" Well, now you know why. You asked for it; you programmed it.

Maxwell Maltz, M.D., a plastic surgeon, wrote a classic book, *Psycho-Cybernetics,* on this subject. Dr. Maltz observed that when he corrected grotesque features, his patients behaved in one of two ways. Some changed their personality and became more outgoing and successful. Conversely, some did not change. They still had an inferiority complex and were failure-oriented.

Dr. Maltz then found he could change some patients from feeling inferior and being failure-oriented *without* surgery. *He concluded that a person's actions, feelings, behaviors, and even abilities, are consistent with his or her self-image.* Therefore, change the self-image and you change the personality and behavior! In other words, *you will act like the sort of person you think you are.* The key to personality change is not physical; it is your self-image.

Dr. Maltz went on to say that the change is not made by intellect, and not by intelligence; change is brought about by *experience.* Remember, experiencing is the same to the subconscious mind as *imagining.* The subconscious mind does not know the difference between real and unreal. It accepts what you feed it. Like the saying, "You are what you eat"; "You are also what you think!" Think of your self-image as the software in your brain, and your neural system as your hardware. Your printout, then, in computer parlance, is your body and your personality.

Your subconscious mind is a goal-seeking computer and will seek whatever you feed it. There are dozens of books on this subject. A classic is *As A Man Thinketh* by James Allen.

It is not so much what you are. More important, it is what you *think* you are. If you continually think of success, your subconscious mind will guide you to success. If you

continually think loving thoughts, your subconscious mind will guide you to loving relationships.

William James said, "The greatest revolution in our generation is the discovery that human beings, by changing the inner attitudes of their minds, can change the outer aspects of their lives."

GOALS

Your goals must be clear, otherwise your subconscious mind will flounder. If you flit from one goal to another, your effort will be inefficient and counterproductive. To keep your goals clear and well thought out, write them down. Keep a record. List short-, medium-, and long-term goals. Suggestions include:

- Better job
- Self-image
- Better place to live
- New house
- Financial independence
- Mental skills
- Physical skills
- Health

Review and revise your goals regularly. I suggest you review them as often as you think of it, even if only for a few seconds. Review them in the alpha state. The entire review will only take a few seconds. Do not share them with anybody. You will likely get negative feedback from well-intentioned friends and family reminding you that you cannot do that, be that, or get that. You will also put pressure on yourself to produce or look foolish. Such pressure will inhibit your success.

ADMONITION

Be certain they are *your* goals. Goals should make *you* happy, while not making anyone else unhappy. Be certain that each sub goal leads to your ultimate goal. Your ultimate goal should be something like: peace of mind, health, and harmony in your life, happiness, and self-fulfillment.

Emerson said, "Be careful what you wish for with all your heart (subconscious mind), for you will surely get it." Your first thought for a goal might be to make lots of money. While making lots of money, you might lose your friends, family, and health, leaving you rich but miserable and lonely. So lots of money may not be the best goal for you. Think your goals out carefully and strike a balance. Always have a clear, definite list that you can refer to (in the alpha state).

SUMMARY OF IMPORTANT SUBCONSCIOUS MIND CHARACTERISTICS

1. Does not know real from imagined.
2. Is always seeking goals.
3. Can be controlled by your conscious mind.
4. Communicates with images and feelings.
5. Communication to the subconscious mind is enhanced with emotion.
6. The alpha state opens the door to the subconscious mind.
7. Keep your conscious mind out of the way:
   - Use no effort
   - Practice detached acceptance
   - Let go!

EXERCISE

SELF-IMAGE

Divide a piece of paper into two vertical columns. Label the left column "Self-Image" and label the right column "Visualization." List three traits in the left column that you want to become. Leave space between. In the right column, list scenarios of what you would be doing provided you had that type of personality. Following is an example:

SELF-IMAGE VISUALIZATION

SELF-IMAGE	VISUALIZATION
• Charismatic	People listening to me People following me Speaking to large audiences
• Excellent Conversationalist	Speaking to a large group Emceeing a talk show
• Successful	Driving my luxury car President of a company Winning a trophy

Keep this piece of paper by your bedside. Just before you lie down to sleep, look at the list and visualize yourself *as already having* these traits. See yourself in action doing those activities and being that person. Do not think of it during the day unless you are in alpha.

Now you have given your genie goals and it will work to see that you successfully achieve them, easily and effortlessly.

THETA CONDITIONING—EXERCISE

The theta state is deep meditation associated with sudden insights where the solution to a problem or a creative effort is often visualized in its entirety. Many examples are described in the literature in which people were working futilely on a problem until they finally gave up (consciously)

and went on a walk, soaked in the bathtub, or engaged in some activity that relaxed them and took their minds off the problem. While they were relaxed and in this meditative state, the solution came to them in a flash. Examples are given in *Higher Creativity,* by W. Harman and other books.

The famous surrealist artist Salvador Dali would sit in a chair, relax, and go in the theta state where he saw the surreal images he painted. Dali would hold some object in his hand so when he reached this inspirational state, his grip would relax and the object would drop. The noise would bring him to a state where he could remember the images he visualized in the theta state.

You do not have to go to that trouble to get into the theta state. You can condition yourself to go into theta anytime you wish by practicing the following exercise. Before you do the theta routine, however, become proficient in going into alpha using the exercise in Lesson Two.[5]

THE INSPIRATIONAL GARDEN ROUTINE

Get comfortable.

Turn your eyes up about 20 degrees. Looking up is fatiguing so allow them to close.

You are always aware of what I am saying.

Allow yourself to relax...allow yourself to become limp. Relaxation is good for you...so let go...just let go and relax. Image you are a balloon, and someone has blown you up and up and up until the balloon is taut and seems ready to explode. There is a valve by your hand. Release it and watch yourself slowly deflate. Down...down...down until you are totally deflated and flat and completely relaxed. Relaxation is associated with feelings of

---

[5] A CD that includes this routine can be purchased at www.TheGenieWithin.net. For more information, contact TheGenieWithin@roadrunner.com or write to *The Genie Within,* 1844 Fuerte Street, Fallbrook, CA 92028.

heaviness and warmth. So now feel your body becoming heavier...and feel a comforting wave of warmth creep across your body....Your legs are now relaxed...completely relaxed...your torso is now relaxed...completely relaxed...your arms are relaxed and limp...feel the weight of your body. Now your head and neck are relaxed...retaining just enough muscle tone to keep your head in a comfortable position. Now imagine you are a bag of cement. Feel how heavy you are. Feel the bag pressing down and down and down.

Now mentally count 3...2...1...and mentally say and see the word "ALPHA." You are now in a natural, healthy state of mind—A state where your subconscious mind readily accepts healthful and positive suggestions, suggestions that are only for yours and humanity's highest good.

Now you are going into an even deeper natural state of mind. Count down mentally from 5 to 1 and as you count allow yourself to go deeper and deeper into this natural relaxed, healthy state...5...you are going deeper...4...more and more relaxed...allow your mind to relax and slip deeper and deeper into the theta state of mind...your mind enjoys this deep state of relaxation and peace of mind. Allow your conscious mind to just be an observer...3...slower and slower, deeper and deeper...2...feeling at peace and restful...1. You are now in the theta state. Your mind is creative and sees things in a global sense.

You are going on a pleasant walk. You are on a flat, soft path covered with soft tree bark. The path winds back and forth, and ahead you see a tall hedge. There is an opening in the hedge, and the path leads through this opening. As you slowly walk through the opening in the hedge, you see the most beautiful garden you have ever seen; there is a profusion of flowers, and it is laid out in perfection, in geometric designs that are pleasing to your eyes. Slowly gaze around and observe the galaxy of flowers. Some have bright colors, some have subdued colors...but they all are beautiful...absolutely gorgeous. There are flowers of all kinds and colors..reds, deep vermilion...delicate pinks. There are blue flowers, deep blue...cerulean blue...azure blues, and greenish blues. There are vivid yellows and spring greens...dark greens and some olive colored flowers. All colors of the rainbow...all shades...greens,

reds, yellows, blues and purples, oranges and violets. Some flowers have large petals...broad and smoothly shaped like a ship's hull...Some flowers are tiny and intricate...they appear delicate, but somehow you know they are hearty. You see much detail in these tiny flowers...such beautiful minute petals.

Being in this garden is an inspiration. Being here in this garden fills you with awe...the beauty is overwhelming. Being here fills you with the desire to create. Such a garden should be enjoyed by all. Being in this realm of truth and beauty inspires you to write a poem...or to write a story...or to paint a picture...to express what you feel in some way...some way that is right for you. Maybe your way of expressing yourself is to help somebody...to do a good deed...to do someone a favor. You will know how to express yourself...happily...effortlessly...joyfully.

Each of these flowers represents something to you. Some represent an idea...or a concept. Some of the flowers represent parts of a story, or parts of a beautiful picture. Some of the flowers represent parts of a speech or a sermon. Others represent acts that you can do for the good of others.

These flowers are limitless. The more you pick, the more they thrive and grow. You may pick as many flowers as you wish. Go ahead and pick some bouquets. Pick large bunches. You may pick many bunches if you wish. And you can always come back for more. They will always be here. Winter, spring, summer, or fall— these flowers grow all year. They are waiting for you to pick them...they want you to pick them because that is what they are here for...your benefit...for your good...to help you fulfill your creative urges.

Now carefully tuck your bouquets under your arms and hold some in your hands. You may even put some flowers in your hair if you desire. Hold them gently...for they are precious...They are your desires manifested into reality...into writings...into stories...into poems...into painted pictures...into quilts or embroideries...into kind acts...into anything that you create. For you are creative...you are productive...you are creating right now.

So as you return to wakefulness, bring these bouquets with you. They are yours to keep forever...they are yours to use...to enjoy for

yourself or to share with friends...or to share with all of humanity. They are yours only to use for your highest good and for humanity's highest good.

You may come to this garden whenever you want. Simply count down from 5 to 1 and visualize the word "THETA." You are now programmed to return whenever you like. Simply count from 5 to 1 and mentally visualize and mentally say to yourself, "THETA." In normal conversation the word theta has no special meaning. Only when you desire to return to "THETA" does the word have any effect. Each time you return to the "THETA" state, it is easier for you to do so. Each time you mentally say the word "THETA," you go down to this level quickly. Each time you go to "THETA," it is easier and easier, and more natural for you to do so.

Now, slowly begin to return to the "awake" state. On the count of 5, you are awake and rested and feeling refreshed. 1...feeling inspired and creative...2...feeling refreshed...3...feeling happy...4...5...you are wide awake.

Lesson Four

LAWS of the Subconscious Mind

Lesson Four

LAWS OF THE SUBCONSCIOUS MIND

INTRODUCTION

The laws of mathematics must be obeyed to get correct mathematical solutions. A correct solution might be obtained on occasion even though a law is disobeyed, but it will not happen often. It is no different with the subconscious mind.

I would like to say that if you obey the laws of the subconscious mind discussed in this lesson, you will always be successful, but no one can make such a promise. However, I can say that if you disobey the laws discussed in this lesson, you will be much less successful than if you *do* obey them. Some of the laws are simple and their explanation is short. I will not embellish on them simply to make the section longer to seem more important.

REPETITION, REPETITION, REPETITION

New programs accepted by the subconscious mind must be nurtured. When programming the subconscious mind, it is necessary to repeat the conditioning often until it is totally accepted by the subconscious mind. After it is accepted, the program should be repeated periodically to ensure that it remains dominant.

EMOTION

Attaching emotion to a suggestion makes it more effective. Emotion is the power in the subconscious mind. You must use it when programming your subconscious mind to be successful.

PRESENT TENSE

The conscious mind lives by time as we know it, namely past, present, and future, whereas the subconscious mind only lives in the present. In the subconscious mind, the past is merely present recollections and the future is present predictions.

The following example explains the significance of using the present tense. "I *will* be happy" infers to the subconscious mind that you are not *now* happy; but you will be happy in the future. First, the future never arrives. So do not ask for something in the future. The future is like the carrot held out in front of someone as something to chase but never catch. Second, the "not happy" implication is the goal given to your subconscious mind. Your subconscious mind then obliges by keeping you unhappy.

The correct phrasing is in the present tense: "I am happy." But you say your pet dog just died, you flunked an exam, you

received an invitation from the IRS, and you are *not* happy! Okay, but if you want to pull out of the doldrums, then you need to say and think, "I am happy—now." "Being happy now" will be the goal given to your subconscious mind. Neurotransmitters travel both ways, from mind to body and body to mind. Once your subconscious mind accepts the concept of "being happy," that message, in turn, is sent to the cells in your body and then your body responds by acting happy.

Using the present tense does seem awkward to the conscious mind, but it is necessary. For example when you programmed your mental alarm clock, you said to yourself, "I am wide awake at seven o'clock," not "I will be awake at seven o'clock."

ONE DOMINANT CONCEPT

The subconscious mind will accept only one concept to be true at any time. More than one concept (thought, habit, program) can be held in the subconscious mind at the same time, but only *one* will be binding. Thus, when the subconscious mind recognizes a concept as true, that concept guides and dominates your actions.

The subconscious mind will only give up on the dominant concept when a stronger, opposing concept is impressed on it. The significance is that a concept cannot be eliminated; it is imbedded in your subconscious mind and your subconscious mind does not forget. A negative concept must be overpowered with a stronger, positive one. The good news is that the source of the concept does not have to be known; it just has to be overpowered with a positive one.

Imagine you are a large balance. Extend both arms out sideways and parallel to the ground. In each hand you hold a balance pan. Imagine you are a "flip-flop" balance—as soon as anything is put on one pan, it drops down all the way. This balance weighs each binding idea you have of yourself on a particular subject. Your right hand has the tray that holds negative concepts, and the left hand has the tray that holds positive concepts about yourself. The balance will flip one way or the other depending on the dominant concept.

Suppose you were brought up in a healthy family environment. Your parents gave you lots of love and nurturing. The self-image you develop is poise and self-confidence. So, these positive concepts go on the left tray and the left side of the balance goes down and stays down. You grow up self-confident.

Conversely, suppose John was brought up in a dysfunctional family environment. John was bombarded with negative stimuli about himself. "You are no good." "You will never amount to anything." "You are a bad boy." "You never do anything right." "You never learn." For the twenty years he lived in this family environment where he was constantly (REPETITION) given these negative affirmations, and much of the time they were said with anger or sarcasm (EMOTION).

Years later John knows (in his conscious mind) he is smart, educated, and good-looking, but for some unknown reason he has a low self-esteem (subconscious mind). When conscious mind and subconscious mind are in conflict, the subconscious mind always wins.

To change this low esteem to self-confidence, John does not have to determine *where* he got his low self-esteem. He simply has to *overpower* his concept of low self-esteem with one of poise and self-confidence. He must give himself positive, healthy, esteem-building affirmations. He must feed the left balance pan until, one day, the balance flips and *voila!* His

subconscious mind has accepted the positive concept. Now self-confidence is the dominant concept guiding John's actions.

John was exposed to years of negative affirmations. How can he overcome this negative trait, which had built up over years, in a short time? He can accelerate the process by programming his positive programs in the alpha state and by using the methods described in later lessons.

William Glasser, M.D. wrote a book, *Schools Without Failure,* suggesting this concept be used in schools. He recommended emphasizing positive and eliminating negative feedback. He suggested there be no condemnation by teachers and no failing grades. He held that children would graduate with higher self-esteems and they would learn faster, easier, and joyfully. This concept has much merit but it was not accepted by our school systems.

This technique for teaching is not used on our children, but it *is* used on animals. Animal trainers are most successful when they ignore negative behavior from the animal and reinforce positive behavior when it occurs. Dr. Skinner, a famous psychologist, was one of the pioneers of this technique.

EXPECTATION

INTRODUCTION

In the previous lesson, you learned that the subconscious mind is a goal-seeking computer. Whatever goals are supplied, the subconscious mind seeks to fulfill them. A sincere *expectation* is a goal given to your subconscious mind, and the law can be stated: *When the subconscious mind expects something, it makes that thing happen.* Here are a couple of examples:

■ Volunteers were inoculated in the right arm with tuberculin from a red syringe. Tuberculin causes

redness and swelling. Consequently, each time the right arm reacted with redness and swelling, as *expected*. At the same time, the volunteers were inoculated in the left arm with a salt solution from a green syringe. No reaction occurred in the left arm, also as *expected*. After three months of inoculations, the tuberculin and the salt solution were reversed in the red and green syringes without the volunteer's knowledge. When they were inoculated with the switched solutions, as *expected* by the volunteers, the right arm reacted with redness and swelling, while the left arm exhibited no reaction. Contrary to medical science, the body reacted according to the *expectation* in the subconscious mind.

■ Sociologists studying the culture in the Torbiand Islands found that premarital sex was considered okay, but premarital pregnancy was not. The natives did not use contraception, yet premarital pregnancy was virtually unknown. The ingrained culture conditioned them so that they absolutely did not expect to get pregnant until they were married.

■ You have probably known or heard of a couple that could not conceive. They adopted a baby and soon after the wife got pregnant. One could argue that having a child unblocked her belief that she could not have a baby of her own.

To reiterate: *Expectation is a self-fulfilling prophecy.*

Now we will examine the most documented phenomenon based on this law—placebos.[1]

---

[1] For more examples see, "The Mysterious Placebo," in *Anatomy of an Illness,* by Norman Cousins, and "Mind Over Medicine," *Psychology Today,* July/August, p.60–67, 2000.

PLACEBOS

The word placebo means, "I shall please." Drug companies must factor in the "placebo effect" when testing every new drug. Placebos are pills that look the same as the medicine being tested but they contain only the inert filler used with the real medicine. This filler has no medicinal value, yet in all studies, at least thirty percent of the patients report the same beneficial results as those who use the real medicine. The placebo effect cannot be explained other than that the patients' *belief* system causes the same healing effect as the real medicine.

When patients are unaware medication is being given to them, the placebo effect disappears. When the patients are unaware, there is no *expectation*. Tests of this nature were run to prove that the placebo effect is truly due to expectation and not another factor.

Dr. Sternbach in 1964 administered a pill containing no active ingredients to a group of volunteers. The first time the pill was given, the group was told that they were receiving a drug that would stimulate a strong churning sensation in their stomachs. The next time, the volunteers were told the pill would reduce stomach activity and make them feel full and heavy. A third time the volunteers were told the pill was a placebo and would serve as a control. Though Dr. Sternbach administered the same pill in all three occasions, *two thirds* of the subjects' stomach activity responded according to the instructions they received before taking the pills. The subjects' stomachs reacted the way the subjects *expected* them to react.

Studies have shown that a patient's belief can be dramatically affected by the way the medicine is dosed. A big pill is more effective than a small one; a colored pill more effective than a white one; a bitter pill more effective than a bland one; an injection more effective than a pill; medication administered by a doctor is more effective than by a nurse, and; medication administered by a doctor in a white coat is more effective than a doctor in street clothes. A patient's belief in the medicine is set up by the way the medication is given. Doctor Benson, in *Timeless Medicine,* stated that placebos can be as much as 90% effective as the real medicine depending on *how* they are administered.

When testing a drug for bleeding ulcers, doctors found that the drug was seventy percent successful when introduced as a "potent" new drug, but only thirty percent successful when introduced as an "experimental" drug.

The importance of the doctor/patient relationship has been reported in recent studies. The placebo effect is stronger when the doctor views patients as active participants, as opposed to the passive just-do-as-I-tell-you relationship.

In an experiment reported by Dr. Joan Borysenko, one-third of women cancer patients given a placebo in place of chemotherapeutic medication lost their hair. The only reason they lost their hair was that they expected to lose hair.

The placebo effect is even effective in surgery. Dr. Bruce Moseley, Jr., used arthroscopic surgery (surgery through small incisions) on five patients, while five others went through a sham surgery in which he made the access cuts but no corrective surgery was performed. Two years later, those who had the sham surgery reported the same amount of benefit from pain and swelling reduction as those who had the real surgery. Four of the people in the placebo group even recommended the surgery to friends.[2]

---

[2] *Vitality* Magazine, Mar., 2002.

Discussion about the placebo effect would be incomplete without the case of Mr. Wright, reported in 1957. Mr. Wright was dying of cancer and his doctor, Bruno Klopfer, M.D., gave him only a few days to live. Mr. Wright found out about a new medicine, Krebiozen, that was being studied at the hospital and he begged Dr. Klopfer to give it to him. Though Dr. Klopfer knew it was too late for any medicine to cure Mr. Wright, he relented and gave Mr. Wright an injection on Friday.

When Dr. Klopfer returned Monday, he wondered if his patient would even be alive. Mr. Wright astounded the doctor by being up and active. Dr. Klopfer reported that Mr. Wright's tumors were "melting like butter on a hot stove." Mr. Wright went home and resumed normal activities until he heard that Krebiozen was not as effective as hoped for. Mr. Wright was soon back in the hospital and dying.

Doctor Klopfer realized it was the placebo effect that was curing Mr. Wright so he told him that the Krebiozen used in the recently reported study was an old batch. The doctor gave his patient another injection telling him he had obtained some fresh Krebiozen. Again the tumors melted like butter on a hot stove and Mr. Wright left the hospital. Another report came out stating that Krebiozen was ineffective and research was abandoned. After hearing of this report, Mr. Wright returned to the hospital and died a few days later.

I will end the placebo effect with a quote from Norman Cousins.[3] Cousins wrote books and taught college graduate courses based on his own healing from a fatal disease using laughter to stimulate his immune system, the inherent healing system in his body. "Over the years medical science has identified the primary systems of the body—circulatory system, digestive system, endocrine system, autonomic nervous system, parasympathetic nervous system, and the

---

[3] *The Mind,* Richard M. Restak, M.D., p160, Bantam Books, 1988.

immune system. But the two other systems that are central to the proper functioning of a human being need to be emphasized—the healing system and the *belief* system. The two work together. The healing system is the way the body mobilizes all its resources to combat disease. *The belief system is often the activator of the healing*" (my Italics.)

REVERSE EFFORT

You cannot sleep. The more determined you are to sleep, the more you wake up.

You are near winning a golf trophy for the first time. There is just one more hole. You tell yourself to ignore the water in front of you. But the harder you try not to think of it, the more you think of it. You choke and your shot goes in the water.

These are examples of The Law of Reverse Effort. The law is subtle but critical. I will explain it in two slightly different ways.

FIRST

Over a century ago Emile Coué wrote: "When *will* (conscious mind) and imagination (subconscious mind) are in conflict, imagination (subconscious mind) always wins." Take the example of trying to recall a name of someone coming toward you. You know her name but it escapes you just now. You are with another friend who you will have to introduce to the woman coming toward you. You *fear* you will be highly embarrassed because you should know the woman's name. Trying to recall her name frustrates you and, the harder you *will* yourself to recall her name, the more frustrated you become. The fear (subconscious mind) of being embarrassed overrides the *will* (conscious mind) to recall the name.

However, the woman passes you and apologizes that she is in a hurry and cannot stop. You are relieved, you relax (you stop imposing your *will*), and her name pops into your head.

Emile Coué described it in mathematical terms to make a point. He said the power of imagination (subconscious mind) is equal to the square of the power of *will* (conscious mind).

Conscious Mind Power^2 = Subconscious Mind Power

$$1 = 1$$
$$2 = 4$$
$$3 = 9$$

Therefore, the more effort you put into your *will*, the more the power of your imagination increases, and at an escalating rate. Thus, the "not remembering" wins. The more you consciously *will* something, the more you increase the opposing power. The trick is to not *will* what you want. The trick is to *let* it happen. Your conscious mind must allow the subconscious mind to do it. Your conscious mind must remain passive and detached.

SECOND

Whenever you *will* yourself to do something, you also harbor a fear of failing. Fear is a powerful emotion. If your fear of failure is stronger than your *will* to succeed, fear wins. The fear of failure is accepted by your subconscious mind and it overpowers your conscious determination to succeed.

Consider the following mental demonstration. Picture a wooden plank four inches wide suspended six inches above

the ground. Go ahead and walk the plank. Easy! Walk it backward and sideways. Easy. Okay, now imagine that same plank is suspended between two skyscrapers 30 stories high. Now walk the plank! It is harder, isn't it? Yet it is the same plank and the same task. But now there is a huge element of fear. "What if I fall? I will be killed! It is frightening to look down. Anybody could slip walking on this narrow piece of wood." No matter how much you *will* yourself to walk across the plank, the fear is stronger. To walk the plank now, you need a high degree of confidence in your ability—enough to *expect* to walk the plank successfully.

You are playing golf and are teeing off in front of a crowd. You want to look good, but you *fear* miss-hitting the ball. The more you *will* yourself to relax and hit the ball 250 yards straight down the fairway, the more tense you become and the more likely you are to slice the ball. Tiger Woods has so much confidence that fear is not a factor. He simply relaxes and hits a successful shot.

To counter the law of reverse effort you must have *faith* to dispel fear and you must *expect* success. At the very least, you must have a neutral attitude. You must resist putting conscious effort into it.

In an advanced Silva International class, I witnessed a demonstration on dowsing. I told my wife about it when I came home and she suggested I repeat the demonstration for her. I was still pumped up from the class and I was confident. If the instructor could do it, I could do it.

First, I went out of the room and my wife hid my car keys. When I came back, I held up one of my dowsing wires and it pointed. I walked in that direction holding both dowsing wires. When I passed over a bucket of Japanese persimmons, the wires crossed. I removed a few persimmons and found my keys. Wow! We were both impressed.

I then asked my wife to imagine a mental wall somewhere in the room. I started walking across the room and when I got to a certain spot the dowsing wires crossed—exactly where she imagined the mental wall. Again, "Wow!"

Next time I lectured, I thought I would give this demonstration. But the following thought came into my head: "If I fail, I will look foolish and the class will lose confidence in me." As you can predict, I could not repeat the dowsing demonstration next time I attempted it. My fear of failure, my fear of losing the confidence of my students (which is so important in this course), won out over my *will* to do a successful demonstration.

EXPRESSION

INTRODUCTION

The Law of Expression states that *every thought causes a physical reaction in the body.*

Close your eyes and imagine biting into a succulent lemon. Your lips pucker and you salivate.

Close your eyes and imagine someone scraping their fingernails across a blackboard. The sound sends shivers down your spine.

Ever read a book, or seen a movie, about a poignant love story and got choked up?

These reactions are examples of the Law of Expression. The mind and body are one: therefore, what affects one affects the other.

Professor William James, a famous psychologist, stated: "The fact is that there is no sort of consciousness whatever, be it sensation, feeling, or idea, which does not directly and of itself tend to discharge into some motor effect. The motor effect

need not always be an outer stroke of behavior. It may be only an alteration of the pulse (heartbeats) or breathing, or a modification in the distribution of the blood, such as blushing or turning pale, or what not. But in any case, it is there in some shape when any consciousness is there and a belief as fundamental as any in modern psychology, is the belief at last attained, *that conscious processes of any sort, conscious processes merely as such, must pass over into motion, open or concealed.*"

Every thought or idea causes a physical reaction. If stimuli are allowed to pass from the conscious mind to the subconscious mind—and are accepted—the idea or thought must be expressed, vocally or physically. If it is consciously repressed, then the thought will be expressed physically, for example:

- Worry = Ulcers
- Anger = Releases adrenaline accompanied by changes in circulation, energy, pulse, and respiration, etc.
- Fear = Nervousness, upset stomach
- Food = Hunger

More than a hundred years ago, a doctor conducted an experiment on a man who was shot in the stomach. The surgeon offered the man room and board in his house if the man agreed to leave the hole into his stomach open for a period so the surgeon could examine the condition of his stomach. By evaluating the stomach secretions, the surgeon found that all moods affected the man's digestion.

In a study conducted at Harvard, Dr. W. B. Cannon found that love, consciously cultivated, caused the eyes to brighten, improved circulation, digestion, and elimination. Whereas, fear, envy, and hate caused the opposite effects. These negative thoughts also cut down on production of red blood cells.

Organ language, discussed in Lesson Three, is also an example of a recurring thought that is expressed organically. Dr. H. F. Dunbar stated in *Emotion and Body Changes,* "Emotion indulged in for a prolonged time actually creates tissue changes in the organ or organ system involved,"

Bailes stated it beautifully in a book written more than 30 years ago, before it was proved scientifically: "Man thinks with his entire body. Every cell has a spark of mind. Man is not a body containing a mind; he is a mind operating through a body! Body is molded by mind. What the mind thinks, the body thinks; that which the body thinks, it becomes."

Bailes related a case he had in which his patient did not like his in-laws, but his wife insisted on walking to their house every Sunday. The patient repressed his dislike, and since every repressed thought has a physical reaction, he developed arthritis to the extent he had an excuse to stay home.

Today there are many books written for the layman on the mind/body link. A few of the well-known authors include, Borysenko, Pert, Dossey, Chopra, and Pelletier. Drs. Pert and Dossey describe in their books how all our cells talk to our subconscious minds.

Remember the old saw, "If you are not happy, act like you are happy and you will become happy." Well, medical science has proven the old axiom. Organic compositions similar to those used by the brain to think are found in all cells. So communication is both ways, i.e., brain to cell, and cell to brain. If you think you are unhappy, you act unhappy. You frown and act glum. But if you act happy when you are sad, the neurotransmitters from the cells in your body travel back to the brain and change its mood to happy.

THE NATURAL ENERGY CYCLE

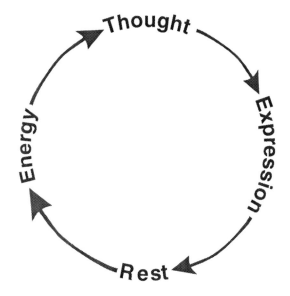

(1) Your body stores *energy*.

(2) The conscious mind gets a strong *thought*.

(3) You *express* the thought.

(4) The body *relaxes* to restore its energy.

Expressed Energy

Look at an age-old example. A caveman wakes after a restful night of sleep. (He has restored his energy.) He sees a saber-toothed tiger browsing outside his cave. He is immediately concerned for the lives of his family and himself. (He has a strong thought.) He gets an adrenaline rush. His body responds with the fight-or-flight reaction. He must defend his family so he elects to fight. After much spear waving and a skirmish, the tiger is driven away. The caveman has

expressed his idea (to fight off the tiger) with *directed action* (fighting the tiger). That evening he is at peace and regains his energy with a night of restful sleep. (The cycle starts over.)

Directed energy is an orderly, healthy release of physical and emotional energy. It is any act that is in harmony with the idea that originated it. Psychologists recommend that when you get mad you should express your anger in some way. Not in a violent way, but in a constructive way. Express it by talking or writing about it or by running around the block, for example. It is unhealthy to bottle up anger. When you do not express it in some way, this emotional energy is *suppressed*.

Suppressed Energy

You are on the freeway driving to an important job interview. Traffic comes to a halt. You are bumper to bumper and no off-ramp is in view. You no longer live in a cave, but you have the same body and response system as your caveman ancestors. When faced with an emergency or unsettling situation, your "fight-or-flight" response kicks into action. The kidneys release adrenaline, heart rate increases, and digestion stops, to name a few of the reactions. Yet all you can do is sit in your car and get more upset thinking about being late for your interview. You imagine  you will lose this fantastic new job. (Remember: Your subconscious mind does not know the difference between real and imagined.)

This energy could be expressed by a primal scream, but the drivers in the cars near you might think you are crazy. If you cannot express the energy at the time your fight-or-flight

response occurs, at least express it as soon as you get a chance. When you get home, you might go for a walk, punch a bag, or clean the house. In this way no, or little, harm is done to your body. The energy is expressed and you can sleep soundly.

Repressed Energy

When an event that triggers your fight-or-flight response occurs continuously, or often, and the energy is not expressed, the energy is *repressed.* Every thought or idea causes a physical reaction. So this repressed energy will be expressed as *undirected* activity, such as tension and anxiety. Tension and anxiety prevent relaxation of the inner muscles, which hinders the immune system and interferes with restful sleep. So, the natural Energy Cycle is broken and restful, restorative sleep is impeded.

CHRONIC STRESS

The body will find a physical outlet for repressed energy, such as fidgeting, nail biting, finger tapping, gum chewing, etc. If it persists, the outlet may become ulcers, high blood pressure, headaches, or worse.

Woody Allen expressed this law another way: "One of my problems is that I internalize everything. I can't express anger; I grow a tumor instead." Surveys of doctors have shown that many believe as much as 90 percent of their patients suffer from chronic fatigue.

Dr. Hans Selye (1907–1982), Professor and Director of the Institute of Experimental Medicine and Surgery, University of Montreal, was first to use the word "stress" in reference to the human body. During 30 years of research, he wrote 1600 papers and 33 books, including *The Stress of Life* for nonprofessionals.

Dr. Selye proved that repressed stress wears the body down until it becomes sick. In his classical experiments,

animals were wired so that they could be given mild electrical shocks. He administered the shocks sporadically so the animals did not know when they were coming. Although the shocks were not severe enough to cause any harm, the *anxiety* of not knowing when they were coming caused *stress*. When this condition went on long enough, the stress impaired their immune system and the animals became vulnerable to disease.

A corollary of this is commonly observed in humans. After a spouse dies and the mate mourns too long, the mate's immune system becomes impaired and he or she becomes ill and often dies.

Other examples were given in Lesson Three, including the woman who after a prolonged resentment of her sister developed breast cancer. This last example points out why it is important to forgive. Forgive, not for the benefit of the transgressor, but for yourself. Harbored resentment breaks the natural cycle and impairs your immune system.

A Dr. McDonald, a coroner, said (in an article that appeared in the *Los Angeles Times* about 30 years ago) he found, when he was looking for it, healed cancer areas in all of the cadavers he ever examined. This implies that we all have cancer cells in our bodies but our immune systems, when healthy and allowed to function properly, prevent their growth. Most of the time, fortunately, cancer cells grow only when the immune system is impaired.

A story from one of James Harriot's books vividly shows the effect of chronic pain and stress. James Harriot was a veterinarian in Yorkshire, England. PBS aired a series for two years called "All Things Great and Small" based on these books.

James Harriot was calling on a miserly farmer. Harriot noticed an ewe that was in obvious pain. A cursory examination showed she had an infected uterus. The farmer

did not want to pay for treating the ewe because he thought she would not survive anyway. Harriot felt obliged to do something for the poor beast so he suggested that he give her some vitamins at no charge.

Harriot did not give the ewe vitamins, instead he gave her what he thought was enough Nembutal, or whatever chemical veterinarians use for euthanasia, to put her out of her misery. Weeks later he met the farmer at a local pub. The farmer told Harriot, "Those vitamins sure did the trick. The ewe slept for three days and when she woke up she was cured."

Harriot thought deeply about the healing and concluded this: Every animal, including man, has the ability to cure itself if given the chance. This poor ewe was in so much pain and fear that her immune system and its curative powers shut down, allowing the infection to flourish. The injection put her to sleep for three days. Asleep, she felt no pain or fear. Without the pain and fear, her immune system took over and cured her naturally. Chronic tension and anxiety interfere with everyone's immune system.

This is why deep relaxation and deep sleep are important. It gives your body an opportunity to regenerate and revitalize itself. Spending eight hours in bed does not necessarily mean you are getting proper sleep. Some people sleep eight hours but get up grouchy and complain of being tired. These people are not getting enough *deep, restful* sleep. They are not fully relaxing the inner core of muscles. These inner muscles are relaxed through your subconscious mind. People who reach deeper levels of sleep need less sleep than those who do not fully relax.

Reaction to Stress

Dr. Selye found that the reaction (the fight-or-flight response, or as he called it, the General Adaptation Syndrome) to stressful stimuli is the same for everyone. But, importantly,

everyone does not react to a given stressful stimulus in the same way.

Take the hypothetical examples of John and Alice who have similar jobs and work for the same boss. The boss is arrogant, grumpy, impersonal, and demanding. John cannot stand the boss and gets upset after every confrontation. Moreover, he gets upset every time he thinks of his job. John constantly complains about his boss and his job. After a year on this job, John has ulcers and high blood pressure.

Alice reacts differently. She analyses the situation and concludes her boss is acting from fear. He is afraid of losing *his* job. He is also having family problems and is probably afraid of losing his wife, or maybe of paying alimony. Once Alice understands this, she realizes that she is not the problem. Knowing this, she does not take his criticisms and grumpiness personally. Alice remains cheerful, productive, and a healthy employee.

To recap, no idea can remain secret in the subconscious mind. Ideas crystallize and must be expressed directly or indirectly.

METHODS OF RELIEVING STRESS

1. *Use the Law of Reverse Effort. Go into alpha and repeat, "Whatever is causing this stress, now acts to relax me."*

2. *Go into the alpha state and visualize a relaxing scene.*

3. *Use the mental overlay method.*

   a. *Write on a piece of paper the thing that is stressing you.*

   b. *Close your eyes. Go into the alpha state. Think of a time when you felt joyful, wonderful, serene, and content. Project this image on your mental screen. Hold it about 30 seconds.*

   c. *Open your eyes and read what you wrote on the piece of paper.*

> **d.** *Repeat steps b. and c, two more times. Now when the thing that used to bug you comes up, you will feel those positive feelings.*
>
> **4.** *Go into the alpha state. If you had a bad experience, replay the experience in a positive way. If you offended someone by saying something you wish you had not said, go over the scene and say the right thing several times. Remember your subconscious mind does not know the difference between real and imagined experiences. This exercise will make it a positive experience, rather than a negative one.*
>
> **P.S.** *You may still want to apologize to the person you offended.*
>
> **Note:** *Do these exercises while sitting in a comfortable chair. Do not do them while driving. Driving a car is okay while in the alpha state as long as you program yourself to drive carefully and alertly. Visualizing being on a tropical island watching swaying palms is not driving carefully and alertly.*

RESISTANCE

A law in physics states: "Any action has an opposite and equal reaction." So to resist is to give the opposite thing power. To resist something that is untrue only puts you on the defensive. A simple example will make the point:

Someone calls you lazy and accuses you of being incompetent. You know you are not lazy or incompetent. When you say, "No, I am not!" you are offering resistance to something that does not exist. You are giving it power and you are putting yourself on the defensive. Now you have to prove you are not lazy and incompetent. You are now struggling against something that is difficult to prove.

On the other hand, when you answer with a simp. such as, "That is true. *You think I am lazy and* incompet. and you have a right to think that. But please tell me why you believe that?" Now the burden of proof is on the other person, and you have defused a potentially violent argument. How can the other person stay mad, or get mad, with an answer like that?

Put your energy on what you stand for and believe in. Do not give your energy to negative causes. I have not studied marshal arts, but I believe one of the axioms is to not resist. A master in the arts does not resist; instead, the master uses an adversary's energy/motion to his advantage.

It is said that Mother Teresa was asked to join an anti-war march. She responded, "No. I will not join your anti-war march but I will march if you have one for peace." And from the Bible, "Resist not evil, but overcome evil with good."

THE TENSE/RELAX CONDITIONING EXERCISE

Dr. Edmund Jacobson introduced the idea of tensing and relaxing in 1938. Each set of muscles in turn is tensed as tight as possible and then relaxed. The purpose is to feel the difference between tension and deep relaxation, and to teach your muscles what you want them to do for you. You want them to relax completely.

Another change in this routine is that the word "sleep" is used. Sleep is not the correct word but there is no other word in the English language to use. In this case, the object is to lose consciousness but not go to sleep, i.e., not to go into the delta state. You will be in the alpha state but your conscious mind will be out to lunch. Your subconscious mind will accept suggestions much more readily because your conscious mind is not there to interfere. This phrase will also be added to the

routine: "In any emergency I am wide awake and alert." This suggestion is really unnecessary because your subconscious mind would wake you if you smelled smoke, heard the baby cry, or whatever. The purpose of adding it in the routine is to remove any apprehension from your conscious mind.[4]

THE TENSE/RELAX ROUTINE

You might want to unwind by stretching your shoulders and neck to improve circulation to the head.

Raise your eyes about 20 degrees and stare at a spot. Your eyelids naturally tire. They first flutter. Now let them close. Your eyes are now closed.

Take a slow, deep breath. Exhale. As you exhale, feel tension beginning to float away and just allow yourself relax. Take a second slow, deep breath, and upon exhaling, feel tension being carried away on the out-breath. Relax. Take a third slow, even, deep breath. Exhale. Imagine tension leaving your muscles. See it leaving. See it fading away. Let yourself relax.

Now, tense your toes as tightly as possible. Curl your toes as tightly as you can. Hold that taut, tense feeling in the toes, 1...2...3. Now, relax your toes. Relax them completely and feel the difference.

Now tense you toes, feet, and the muscles in the lower part of the legs. Make those muscles very, very tense, but keep the rest of your body relaxed. Hold that feeling of tension 1...2...3. Now relax. Enjoy that feeling of release from tension.

Now tense the muscles in the upper apart of the legs as well as the muscles in the toes, feet, and lower legs. Make those muscles as tense as possible. Tense them a little bit more. Feel that tension with your body and mind, 1...2...3. Now relax. Feel those muscles unwinding and letting go, unwinding and letting go. Now tell those muscles to relax even more. Feel your muscles getting heavy.

[4] A CD that includes this routine can be purchased at www.TheGenieWithin.net. For more information contact TheGenieWithin@roadrunner.com or write to *The Genie Within,* 1844 Fuerte Street, Fallbrook, CA 92028.

Now tense your buttocks muscles. Hold that tension, 1...2...3. Now relax. Feel yourself getting heavier and heavier. Heavier and heavier. Feel the pleasantness of deep relaxation. Feel a wave of joy come over you.

Now tense the muscles in your lower back and abdomen. Note how it feels to have your body all wound up with tension. Tense those muscles even more tightly, 1...2...3. Relax, unwind, let go, and relax.

Let the tension drain out of every muscle. Let go of all your weight. Allow your body to relax those muscles a little bit more. Note what this sensation of relaxation is like.

Now tense the muscles in the upper part of your torso. Hunch both shoulders. Tense the muscles in the chest and back. Make those muscles even tenser. Really feel that tension, 1...2...3, and relax. Exhale and feel all those muscles in your chest and back relaxing. Feel all those muscles relaxing, unwinding, and letting go. Feel all the tightness and tension disappearing. Let those muscles relax a little bit more. Recognize what a wonderful feeling it is to relax.

Now tense your arms and clench both fists. Really feel that tension, 1...2...3. Now relax. Let your arms flop to your sides. Enjoy the release from tension.

Next, squinch all the muscles of your face. Tense every muscle in the face that you can. Tense your jaw. Clench your teeth, tighten your scalp, squint your eyes. Hold it, 1...2...3, then relax. Smooth out all the muscles of the forehead, relax your scalp, relax your eyes, relax your mouth, tongue, and throat. Remove all strain and tension. Relax all your facial muscles. Really feel the difference.

Now tense every muscle in the entire body. Start with your toes, work up to your legs, your abdomen and back, chest and shoulders, arms and fists, neck and face. Be as tense as you can. Clench every muscle in the entire body. Hold that tension, 1...2...3. Now relax. Let it go. Relax. Unwind. Really let go. Feel the pleasant relaxing feeling spreading over your entire body. Feel a comfortable, pleasant sensation of relaxation. Note how it feels to be completely relaxed.

Now with your mind's eye, mentally scan your body from head to toe. Rid your body of any residual tension that might be left over. Your body is now completely relaxed.

Let the pleasant sensation of relaxation flow through you from head to toes and back up again. Really enjoy it. Notice how complete relaxation feels. Waves of relaxation flow freely from head to toe and back up again.

Listening to my words is unimportant. Just let go...let go.

Now see yourself standing at the top of a flight of stairs. They descend gently before you. Upon each step there is painted a number. "10" is painted on the top step and the numbers decrease with each descending step. Now slowly descend these stairs one at a time as you count backwards. With every count, you become drowsier and drowsier as you relax more and more...deeper and deeper. Allow yourself to drift, float and drift down into pleasant, relaxing rest. When you reach step "1" you are in a deep, deep natural sleep. These steps are easy and safe. There are handrails on both sides. Now descend to step "9," and as you do you feel heavier and drowsier. Now step down to "8" and as you do you relax even more. Now step "7" and "6." You feel drowsier and drowsier. Now descend to step "5" and you are deeper and deeper asleep. Notice it is getting darker and you are feeling heavier and...oh...so heavy. Your legs are sluggish...they are so heavy. "4," deep and deeper...darker and darker. You are relaxed and comfortable and completely safe. You are completely safe. Go down to step "3." You are calm and at ease. You are drifting into complete relaxation...complete rest. "2"...mind and body at rest...your mind and body are working together for you highest good. "1," deep asleep...deep asleep. Allow your mind to drift into beautiful, safe, landscapes. Enjoy the feeling of complete relaxation. Your mind is now open to suggestions...only healthful, positive suggestions that are only for your highest good...only for the highest good of humanity.

Each time you practice relaxing, it is easier and faster for you. Each time it is easier. Each time you relax, you go deeper and deeper.

Each time you want to relax and attain this deep state of sleep, simply say to yourself, and see the word, "RELAX." Thinking and visualizing the word "RELAX" allows you to quickly reenter this state of mind. Each time you say the word "RELAX" with the intention of going into a deep hypnotic sleep, you do so quickly, easily, safely, and with peace of mind. You do it easily, quickly, and safely. Going to this deep state of mind allows you to program healthful attitudes and healthful habits that are for your good. It allows your conscious mind and subconscious mind to work together for your best health and mental condition. Saying or thinking the word "relax" during normal conversation is ineffective. Only when you intend to go into this deep state of mind does the word have this effect on you.

Now begin to return to your awake state. You mind is returning to its natural awake state. You are going to count to "10" and be fully awake. You are wide-awake on the count of "10." You may return to this enjoyable state any time you wish. But now you are awake on the count of "10." "1"..."2"...beginning to wake..."3"...bring this feeling of joy and happiness with you..."4"..."5"...feeling refreshed..."6"...feeling wonderful... "7"...feeling energized..."8"..."9"..."10"...you are WIDE AWAKE!

COMMUNICATING
With Your
Subconscious Mind

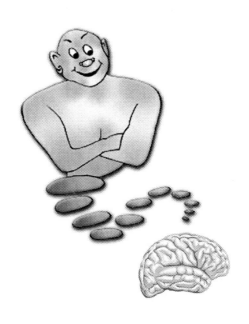

Lesson Five

COMMUNICATING WITH YOUR SUBCONSCIOUS MIND

INTRODUCTION

The lack of or poor communication between our conscious minds and subconscious minds is the cause of many of our problems. This was pointed out in Lesson Two. Thus, developing and nurturing communication between your conscious mind and subconscious mind is imperative. Five techniques for communicating with your subconscious mind are presented in this lesson. The first method is especially important and should be practiced all the time. The second method is also useful and many people use it daily. The third and fourth methods can be very useful but are not something you would normally do every day. The last method may be the most important. Psychiatrists, family doctors, and other health practitioners use it to find the cause of physical and emotional problems, test for allergies, and determine the value and dosages of vitamins, herbs, and medications.

Developing communication between your conscious mind and subconscious mind is a critical step in making your conscious mind and subconscious mind work in concert. If they are not in concert, the subconscious mind, rather than

your conscious mind, will likely prevail. Your genie is not supposed to be in charge.

INTERNAL CONVERSATION

We constantly talk to ourselves in our mind. In fact, quieting the mind is difficult. This talk is usually just chatter. The conscious mind is doing the talking, but who is it talking to? To itself or to the subconscious mind? It can be either, but I believe 99 percent of the time, it is conscious mind talking to conscious mind. It is usually meaningless "monkey talk."

But there are times when you need to talk to your subconscious mind so you need to be specific. Suppose I was ready to give a lesson; it was time to start; I walked up to the lectern; opened my brief case, and; found I left my notes at home. In panic, I could say to myself, "Relax, Harry. Relax, and take it easy. You know the lesson material. Just relax and outline it in your head. You can do it. It will be easy." Recall the Law of Reverse Effort. The harder I will myself to recall the lecture outline, the harder it is to recall it.

If I want to relax and recall the outline, I am wasting time talking to Harry. Harry is my conscious mind. My data bank (memory) is in my subconscious mind. Also, I am wasting time asking my conscious mind to relax. Deep relaxation is controlled by my subconscious mind. Okay, so I should talk to my subconscious mind. So I say, "Hey! You there! Subconscious

mind. Genie. Get to work. Relax my body and my nerves and bring up the outline of my lesson and do it now!"

That way of asking is not friendly. Your goal is to develop a rapport with your subconscious mind—your genie. You want to be friendly and appreciative. You want to open dialog and work together. What is the first thing you need when you talk to a friend? The friend's name! When you are friendly with someone and working closely together, you use first names. So, if you want to be friendly with your subconscious mind, your subconscious mind needs a name. The way to obtain a name for your subconscious mind is explained in an exercise below.

When you want something from your subconscious mind, ask it in a nice, but firm way. (Remember, your subconscious mind is not as emotionally mature as you are.) Become friendly with it. After all, it is part of you and the two of you must work together for your best good. When it grants your request, thank it! Why not? When someone does something for you and you do not thank him or her, they may not be so willing to do something for you again. From now on you have a real friend in your subconscious mind and you are going to treat that friend with respect and love.

Getting back to my dilemma of forgetting my lecture notes, my conversation with my subconscious mind would go something like this. "Oh boy, Ralph (that is the name my subconscious mind picked out for itself) I forgot my notes. Listen, we have given this lecture dozens of times and you and I know it by heart. You and I are perfectly relaxed and we are relaxed throughout the lecture. (I am using the present tense.) I trust you to feed me all I need to know in the correct sequence. I can already see the lecture outline unfolding as I need it. So let's act as if the notes were right here and get on with the lecture. We can do it together and I really appreciate your help. Thank you for always being so helpful. I love you."

NAMING YOUR SUBCONSCIOUS MIND

Go into alpha or do this exercise just before falling asleep at night when your subconscious mind is open and receptive to your suggestions.

Say to yourself something like this: "Subconscious mind, from now on, you and I are a team working together for our mutual good. Being in excellent physical and mental conditions are of benefit to both of us. From now on you and I are best friends. From now on, we communicate more and when I talk to you I want to call you by name—a name you like. You can select your own name. You are to select a name for yourself by ___Mommy___ *(make a definite deadline or your subconscious mind may procrastinate)."*

You may want to also consider the following. First, the name should not be one with strong emotional connotations, such as a family member's or an ex-spouse's name.

Second, tell your subconscious mind to give you this name in a way you can understand. Subconscious minds can be playful and yours may tease you by giving you only hints. Maybe it wants to be called Silvia. So you might consciously notice everything you see that is colored silver. For some reason, you might start noticing silver cars. When you look in a mirror you might recall that the backside of the mirror is silvered. You might get the urge to polish your silverware. You probably will not realize these thoughts are your subconscious's way of letting you know it selected the name of Silvia.

Normally a name will come to mind naturally. You probably will not give it any thought at first but it will persist. That is the name your subconscious mind has selected.

The name can be verified, if you have any doubt, by using the next method of talking to your subconscious mind.

PENDULUM

DESCRIPTION

A pendulum can be made by tying any small weight on about nine inches of thread. The weight can be a finger ring, metal washer, or small crystal, for example. Hold the end of the thread gently between your thumb and forefinger. Rest your  elbow in front of you on a table. The direction the pendulum swing signifies the answer to your question.

There are four ways your subconscious mind can swing the pendulum: clockwise, counterclockwise, east to west, and north to south.

And there are four standard answers: "Yes," "No," "I do not know," and "I do not wish to answer that question." The last answer is for those who delve deeply into the subconscious mind. Some things in your subconscious mind are hidden from you for your own good. You should not dig into your subconscious mind that deeply without professional guidance.

The pendulum works, according to some, for the same reason there is validity in handwriting analysis. There seems to be an open channel for electrical impulses to travel from your subconscious mind to your fingers used for writing, the same fingers used for holding the pendulum. Lefties should experiment with both left and right hands to see if one works better.

The pendulum is used in the following manner. Sit and rest your elbow on a table. Hold the loose end of the thread gently between your thumb and forefinger. The weight should be suspended by about eight or so inches of thread. Bend your elbow enough to let the pendulum swing freely. Ask your subconscious mind to select one of the four signals for a "Yes." You might close your eyes so there is less likelihood of your conscious mind overriding your subconscious mind. Also, it is best if you put yourself in the alpha state when you use the pendulum. The alpha state opens the door to the subconscious mind and subdues the conscious mind so it does not interfere.

If, when you open your eyes, the pendulum is not swinging, firmly command your subconscious mind to select one of the four signals to mean "Yes" and command that it swing the pendulum, and to swing it in wider and wider movements. I have never seen anyone fail.

After your subconscious mind has selected a signal for "Yes," ask it to select one for "No." Then repeat the procedure for "I do not know." The fourth answer is not needed.

QUESTIONS

There are a few points to remember in asking your subconscious mind questions. Your subconscious mind takes things literally so phrase your questions precisely. Keep an open mind (conscious mind). Do not think of what the answer might be or what you would like it to be. Stay neutral.

Lecron reported that 90 percent of the 381 pregnant women that used the pendulum to determine the sex of their unborn baby (this was prior to the availability of modern testing methods) were correct. Many of those women who erred admitted that they had a strong conscious desire for the sex they predicted. Your conscious mind can override results. So rather than think (conscious mind) "I sure hope it is a little

girl!" when using the pendulum, stay neutral by thinking, "I wonder what my baby's sex will be?"

Bird hobbyists use pendulums to determine the sex of newborn chicks. Sex cannot be determined visually so an alternate method is required. You can test this right now. Hold your pendulum over a female. The pendulum will swing in circles. Hold it over a male and it will swing back and forth. The pendulum is useful for many things, for example:

- Checking hunches
- Dream interpretation
- Vitamin dosages
- Allergy sources
- Source of gut feelings
- Reason for procrastination
- Origin of illness

The items listed below can be helpful in determining the cause of an illness:

- Conflict
- Motivation
- Suggestion
- Organ language
- Identification (with someone else)
- Self-punishment (guilt)
- Past experience
- Need for attention
- Need to control someone

Questions you might ask your subconscious mind, for example, are:

- "Is this illness due to a conflict I have with someone or between my conscious mind and subconscious mind?"
- "Is there motivation serving to protect me in some way?"
- "Is this illness due to a suggestion my subconscious mind has accepted as true?"
- "Is (the problem) due to organ language?"
- "Is there a purpose this illness is serving?"
- "Am I seeking sympathy and attention?"
- "Is it preventing me from doing something I do not want to do?"
- "Is it preventing me from doing something that is harmful to me?"

Before I retired, I used to get two colds every year. These colds were severe enough that I had to stay home. Since I retired eight years ago, I have had only one cold, even though I have ample opportunities to get them from more frequent contacts with grandchildren. I became curious about this change and came up with a theory. I considered it a sin to take time off work even though there were times I desperately needed a break. Maybe my subconscious mind gave me a cold to justify taking time off work without feeling guilty. I asked my subconscious mind if this was true and it responded, "Yes."

The pendulum method is an easy way to talk to your subconscious mind. Nevertheless, it does take some ingenuity since you have to work with only "yes" and "no" answers. Think of it as a game, a game like the old TV show, "Twenty Questions."

FINGER MOVEMENT

Suppose you are in a restaurant giving your order to the waiter. You want the pork with the rich cream sauce but your stomach has been upset lately. So you are not sure the pork is right for your stomach. Ask your subconscious mind if it is okay to order the rich pork plate. You can do that with your pendulum, but the waiter, not to mention other patrons, might think you are crazy. You might also be so self-conscious you will not get the correct answer. Use the "finger movement" method and no one will be the wiser.

Comfortably place your dominant hand on the table in front of you. Explain to your subconscious mind that there is another method for responding with the "Yes," "No," and "I do not know" answers. Command your subconscious mind to lift one of your four fingers for a "Yes." The response will probably not be dramatic but one of your fingers will gently lift off the table. Command your subconscious mind to select another finger for a "No," and a third finger for "I do not know."

Now you can inconspicuously converse with your subconscious mind in public without any one knowing.

INDUCED DREAMING

DESCRIPTION

Your subconscious mind works 24 hours every day. Since it is awake at night and can do trillions of things at a time, you might as well give it a job. Put it to work solving a problem or coming up with a new idea. By problems, I do not mean personal problems because you do not want to *worry* while you sleep. I mean constructive problems like:

- How to decorate your living room,
- How to landscape your front yard,

- (If you are a student) how you can find more time to study,
- (If you are an architect) how to design the perfect house for your client,
- (If you are a writer) how to develop a story line for your book,
- How to get more people to join your new club,
- Etc.

Friedrich A Kekulé, a German scientist, was frustrated by a problem he (his conscious mind) worked on for years. The problem was how carbon atoms combined in the benzene molecule. None of his concepts met the scientific criteria. While asleep, when his conscious mind was out of the way, he dreamed of snakes. These snakes acted abnormally—they were chasing their tails, and when a snake caught its tail, it went around in circles. On awakening, Kekulé recalled the dream and it hit him. He had an "Aha" experience. He had not thought of that possibility before. Of course, the carbon atoms in benzene form a ring. The scientist won a Nobel Prize for defining the structure of the benzene molecule.

Steve Allen made the most money he ever made on a song he heard in a dream. He needed a song for the opening of a musical, *The Bachelor*. Consciously, he was not having luck coming up with a song. Remember, your subconscious mind is a goal-seeking computer. He gave his subconscious mind the goal, the need for a smash hit song with a particular theme, but his conscious mind was probably getting in the way due to the pressure. One night he dreamed of the song he needed and wrote it down when he woke up. The song was, "This Could Be the Start of Something Big."

For years, Elias Howe worked on perfecting the sewing machine but he could not solve one sticky problem. One night he dreamed savages were chasing him. They caught him and dragged him to their king. The king ordered Howe to produce

the sewing machine within 24 hours or they would kill him. Howe could not meet the deadline and as the savages were about to kill him, he noticed their spears had small eye-shaped holes at the spear *tips*. That was the solution to his longtime problem—putting the eye of the sewing needle at the *opposite* end of the traditional needle.

In the 1700's guns fired shot. The process of hand casting shot was slow and expensive. Thus, shot was limited in supply. (Maybe that was a good thing!). James Watt worked on ways of increasing production of shot with his conscious mind but could not come up with any practical ideas. Then he had a dream. He was walking in a rainstorm and the raindrops, instead of splattering, remained spherical when they hit the ground. Aha! He woke with the idea of lead rain that solidified before the drops hit the ground. He devised a way of creating molten lead rain. He poured molten lead through a sieve from a tall building. The drops of molten lead solidified in the air and dropped on the ground as pellets, all the correct size. Making lead shot was changed over night from slow and expensive to fast and cheap.

An article in the Jan/Feb, 1996 issue of *Intuition* magazine reported on interviews with fiction writers who obtain much of their writing material in dreams. The reporter got the idea for the article from one of her dreams.

One writer was Sue Grafton, the well-known mystery writer. Grafton said: "I reach a point in many of my books, when I'm very heavily engaged in the process of writing (conscious mind) where I have a problem I can't solve. As I go to sleep I will give myself the suggestion that a solution will come...I know that I will waken and the solution will be there. I know when the analytical self finally releases its grip on us and gets out of the way, the creative side of us, which often surfaces in sleep, comes to the fore and in its own playful and whimsical manner solves many creative problems."

"If I am blocked or very confused or frustrated, I will drink coffee late in the day, knowing that it's going to wake me up in the dead of night. So I get to sleep perfectly soundly and then, at three A.M. when left brain (she is referring to her logical brain, her conscious mind) is tucked away, not being vigilant, right brain (she is referring to her subconscious mind) comes out to play and helps me...I write letters to right brain all the time (she has a good, friendly, relationship with her subconscious mind!)...And the right brain, who likes to get little notes from me, will often come through within a day or two...All of the humor in my books (subconscious minds are playful) comes from Kinsey (Grafton has a name for her subconscious mind)."

"In order to get in touch, I have to block out ego (conscious mind). Ego is the piece of me that's going, 'How am I doing, champ?' 'Is this good?' 'Do you like this?' 'Do you think the critics will like this?' That has nothing to do with creating...So I need to work from within...And that's a question of not being self-conscious, not being cute, not thinking I'm so hot. Not thinking anything, not making judgments about myself. Not sitting critiquing myself, but being still enough to hear the voice that tells me what I'm supposed to do next."

"I think if you tell your unconscious to give you information in your dreams, it will oblige you. It's really amazing how the unconscious longs for ways to get in touch with us. And dreams are a perfect way to do it, because they often seem so unrelated to our conscious worries."

METHOD

The way to use induced dreaming is simple. Just before you fall asleep, tell your subconscious mind to give you the answer to your question, or come up with an idea or solution to a problem, in a dream...in a dream *this* night...in a dream that you *remember* and *understand.*

Have pencil and paper ready. When you wake, the dream may be vivid and you think you will remember it later. However, when your subconscious mind fades as your conscious mind wakes, the dream may fade as well.

If you are not certain about your interpretation of a dream, ask your subconscious mind for verification using your pendulum.

AUTOMATIC WRITING

DESCRIPTION

At some time, you have found yourself doodling, that is, drawing figures unconsciously while talking on the phone or during some other distraction. Automatic writing is the same thing but the subconscious mind expresses itself by writing rather than drawing.

Everyone is capable of automatic writing but people differ in proficiency. Some people write backwards, upside down, or mirror wise. Most write childlike. Remember, this is your subconscious mind expressing itself. It is immature, playful, and illogical. So do not expect to see your normal (conscious mind) penmanship.

People have written stories, poetry, composed music, developed designs, etc. by automatic writing. Ruth Montgomery, a successful author, claims her books are written by her subconscious mind. *Conversations With God, I, II,* and *III,* were written, according to the author, Neal Donald Walsch, by God. Most people may not believe that God literally wrote his books, but if it was not God, then, at least, the writing was through his subconscious mind.

A Course In Miracles was allegedly written by Jesus. You may not believe that Jesus was the author, but the content was definitely not from the conscious mind of the person who

wrote the words, Helen Schucman, a Professor of Medical Psychology at Columbia University's College of Physicians and Surgeons in New York City. Professor Schucman was Jewish, an atheist, and conservative in theory. Her conscious mind could not write such a book.

Jane Roberts was writing poetry one day and something took over her pen and she began the writing automatically about ideas that were completely foreign to her. These writings can be read in the book *Seth Speaks*.

METHOD

Automatic writing is easy. These instructions are meant as a guide since everyone may respond differently.

1. Use a wide body pen.
2. Hold it vertically, either between finger and thumb, or by making a fist around it.
3. Rest your elbow lightly on the table so that it is free to move. You could even put your forearm in a sling for freer motion.
4. Write on an extra large sheet of paper.
5. I suggest you go into the alpha state. This does not seem necessary for most people, evidently, because none of the books I read on this subject mentioned the need to go into an altered state of mind. Maybe they did go into an altered state but were not aware of it.
6. Command your subconscious mind to write.
7. Do not look at the paper. Keep your conscious mind out of the way.
8. If your subconscious mind is slow to start, consciously just start the pen moving.

9. Sometimes switching hands helps.
10. Distract your conscious mind. Watch TV, or listen to music.

MUSCLE RESPONSE TESTING

Your subconscious mind communicates with your organs and every cell in your body. Therefore, it knows what is right and what is wrong with your body, emotionally, chemically, and physically. Problems are known at the cellular level long before they manifest at the physical level. This cellular information can be accessed by "Muscle Response Testing" (MRT), also called "Kinesthesiology" and "Applied Kinesthesiology" testing. MRT is a proven method used by therapists, chiropractors, and doctors.

MRT is based on the facts that positive energy strengthens muscles and negative energy weakens them, and that the truth is associated with positive energy and untruths with negative energy. Any muscle can be tested but traditionally the deltoid muscle is used. The subject holds one arm out sideways parallel to the ground. The subject is asked to resist and the tester pushes down with light pressure on the outstretched wrist using two or three fingers. The shoulder is locked and cannot be budged. The subject or the tester makes a statement. When the answer is true, the deltoid muscle is strengthened and again the arm does not move. When the answer is false, the muscle weakens noticeably and the arm gives under the light pressure by the tester.

The method described above requires two people to perform the test. Variations can be used so that only one person is required. One method is to form interlocking circles with the thumb and forefinger of each hand. Make a statement and then pull your hands apart. If the statement is true, your

fingers will remain locked and cannot be pulled apart. If the statement is false, your fingers will weaken and break apart.

There are a few subtleties to this test so it is helpful to get lessons from an expert if you can. A few of the subtleties, according to some teachers, include:

- Jewelry should be removed, especially watches, before testing.
- Music should not be played while testing.
- The statement must be kept firmly in mind while testing.
- After you or your partner makes the statement, one of you should say, "resist."
- If you are weak or feeling negative, your answers may be tainted.

MRT can be used to:

- Determine whether a substance is beneficial or harmful to you.
- Determine the best dosage of a vitamin, herb, or medication for you.
- Determine whether you have a vitamin or mineral deficiency.
- Determine the health of specific organs.
- Find the source of an illness.
- Find out how your subconscious mind feels about a concept.
- Find the origin of a fear or the source of anxiety.

I will give you a few examples and then you can test yourself. First, make a true statement, "My name is _____ ." You will test positive. Now say, "My name is Milford." You will test negative, unless your name *is* Milford.

Think of Abraham Lincoln and George Washington. You

will test positive. Then think of Adolph Hitler and Josef Stalin. You will test negative. (If you test positive, see a therapist.)

Hold a healthful substance to your solar plexus, such as a capsule of organic vitamin C, and then do the MRT. You will test positive. Now repeat the test but use white sugar. You will test negative.

Hold the image of the vitamin C capsule in your mind and say, "500 milligrams is the best dosage for me." If you test negative, use another amount and repeat the test until you find the optimum dosage of vitamin C for you.

Repeat the above test using any medication you are taking. If you think you like a colleague, say her name is Sally, but there is something uneasy about your relationship, test for, "I like Sally; I think of her as a good friend." You will probably test positive. Ah, but that was the truth for your conscious mind. Now test your subconscious mind. "I like Sally at a subconscious level and my subconscious mind thinks of her as a friend." If you test negative you now know why you have an uneasy feeling about Sally.

MRT was pioneered by George Goodheart, M.D. He found that the strength or weakness of muscles was connected to the condition of body organs. Dr. Goodheart called the technique "applied kinesiology." Three books were published ca. 1971 in which he was a coauthor, but they are out of print.

In the late 1970's, John Diamond, M.D., a psychiatrist, refined the technique and called it "behavioral kinesiology." He found that muscles weaken or strengthen in the presence of positive or negative emotional and intellectual stimuli, as well as physical stimuli. He published his findings in *Behavioral Kinesiology,* in 1979, and in *Your Body Doesn't Lie,* also in 1979.

David R. Hawkins, M.D., Ph.D., also a psychiatrist, advanced the method to significantly higher levels. He made two giant contributions. One, he verified the consistency of

test results by having hundreds of subjects of all ages, ethic backgrounds, and professions test the same statements independently and get the same results. Two, he broadened the scope of testing which I cannot begin to describe here. I highly recommend his books, *Power vs. Force,* and *The Eye of the I.* He also coauthored a notable book with Nobelist Linus Pauling, *Ortomolecular Psychiatry.*

I witnessed an amazing example of the power of MRT. Several medical specialists diagnosed a friend, we will call her Martha, as having an incurable bladder disorder. Martha was in discomfort, overweight, and taking several potent medications. Since the doctors could not cure her, and this would be a lifelong illness, they referred her to a support group. Instead of giving up and going to the support group, she went to see Valerie Moreton Gersch, the founder of KALOS, an organization that teaches MRT. Using MRT, Valerie discovered that Martha was allergic to several common foods and had some imbalances in her system. After three months on a restricted diet and taking a few herbs, she was completely cured, at her normal weight, and in excellent health. Valerie has written two books on MRT that can be purchased through KALOS (1-800-775-2567.) Another informative book on this subject is *Energy Medicine* by Donna Eden, 1998.

"ALERT" CONDITIONING PROGRAM

There are times when being alert is essential. Maybe you feel sluggish or tired, but you have to take an exam or attend an important meeting. The following program conditions you to wake up and become alert at any time and under any circumstance. The trigger word is "ALERT." Whenever you want to become attentive and alert, count down from 10 to 1 and say and think the word "ALERT." Your mind and body will be stimulated and you will be ready for action.

"ALERT" PROGRAM

Get comfortable. Look up about 20 degrees and stare at a spot. It is a strain to look up and your eyelids are beginning to tire. Allow your eyelids to slowly close. Your eyes are now closed.

You are beginning to relax...you are letting go...letting go. All the stress in your body dissipates and is released. Become aware of your muscles from head to foot. Scan your body and relax any muscle that might still have some tension in it. Relaxing is soooo easy...just let go and become limp...limp. Mentally count down from 5 to 1. 5...you are more and more relaxed. 4...every muscle in your body is totally relaxed. Visualize a pile of rubber bands. Take one of them and stretch it, let it go, and let it fall on the floor. See how it releases all tension and becomes completely relaxed...just as you are now. 3...and 2...you are feeling warm and heavy and very relaxed...1..."RELAX." You are now in a deep sleep and in a healthy, natural state of mind...a healthy state...you relax even more each time you exhale.

You are in a state of mind where your conscious mind and your subconscious mind work together in harmony for your highest good. Your subconscious mind and your conscious mind love each other and always work for your best health and mental well-being. They communicate with each other continually...working in harmony...working for your perfect health and mental well-being. They each do this lovingly and happily. Your subconscious mind readily takes positive, healthy, constructive orders from your conscious mind and, as long as they are for your highest good, and do no one else harm, carries out each command swiftly and lovingly. Your increasing mental faculties are for serving yourself and humankind better.

Nothing can disturb your present state. Everything around you aids you in maintaining this deep state of mind.

Now imagine you are visiting Boulder Dam on the Colorado River. You are standing in the middle of the dam, which is more than 1200 feet long. It is massive. Look out in one direction and you see Lake Mead, the largest man-made lake in the world. Look in the other direction and you are looking down into the Colorado River where it flows out of the dam. You are looking down 726

feet. It is scary to look down. It is more than 44 stories tall and it holds back a virtual sea of water. Notice the many thick power lines that lead away from the dam to Los Angeles, Las Vegas, and other cities.

You are going down into the power–generating room that is deep down at the base of the dam. You enter an elevator and you notice your subconscious mind is the operator. You command your subconscious mind to go down to the power-generating room near the bottom of the dam. You begin to descend...from the first floor...down...down...you can feel the lightness in your body due to the acceleration of the elevator. You feel yourself going deeper and deeper to sleep...deep, restful sleep...deeper...deeper. You feel the anticipation of witnessing the huge power generators. The elevator begins to slow in preparation for stopping at the bottom of the dam. You are expecting something gigantic...something wonderful...something helpful...something powerful. The elevator comes to a stop.

The elevator opens and you see a large room, at least two football fields long. Ten huge electrical generators are lined up along the room. Each must be 10 feet in diameter and 10 feet high. And each has thick power lines that transmit the electrical power to the cities where it is needed. In front of you is the control panel to the 10 generators. Each generator has its own switch, and a meter shows the total power output for the ten generators.

Turn on generator number 1. Hear the whine of the rotors as the turbine begins to rotate...faster and faster. You see the meter needle jump to 1 on a scale of 10. There is a pleasant warmth flooding through your body. With each higher number the effect doubles...channeling greater amounts of power to every cell and fiber in your body. You remain relaxed, but ready for action. Now turn on generator 2. The whine of the rotors is even louder as the two generators produce power. Turn on generator 3 and then 4. Now you can feel the intense vibration on the floor as four generators spin. You see the needle on the meter jump to 4. You feel the tingling of energy but you remain relaxed. Turn on generator 5. The noise gets louder...turn on generators 6 and 7. The noise is almost unbearable. Put on the ear protectors that

are placed in front of you. The ear protectors help, but the noise is still loud. And the vibration is even shaking the walls. You inhale strength...and power...and energy...and vitality with each breath. Turn on generators 8...and 9. I have to scream at you to hear me...yet your body remains limp but poised. Power is pulsing throughout your body. The vibration is so pronounced that you have trouble holding on to switch number 10. Turn on the 10th generator and you are now at full power. The meter needle pegs out at 10 and the dial glows alert red. You are now fully ALERT and ready for any condition that confronts you. You are pulsating with dynamic energy.

You can feel adrenalin pulsing through your body...you can feel the tremendous energy tingling in your entire body...You are now fully ALERT and ready to tackle any task with focused attention and boundless energy. You feel wonderful and powerful. Ready for anything. You are in complete control. You know you can control your body and your actions. You are ready for action. Ready now...on the count of 10 and the signal of the word "ALERT," open your eyes...1-2-3-4-5-6-7-8-9-10—ALERT!!! Eyes wide open!

METHODS of Using Your Subconscious Mind, Part 1

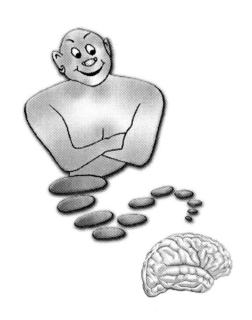

Lesson Six

⟶ REVIEW OF KEY POINTS

EXPECTATION

When the subconscious mind expects something, it tends to bring that thing about. Expectation is a self-fulfilling prophecy. You must expect results when you give your subconscious mind commands. The examples given in the first lesson prove the power of your subconscious mind. You have the capability. So expect positive results. Your genie will respond.

Since you expect positive results, do not be surprised when you get them. Of course, your genie came through! You expected it! Just say "thank you." Surprise shows lack of confidence. Thankful acceptance shows confidence.

POSITIVE ATTITUDE

Keep a positive attitude. Even if results do not occur on your (conscious mind) time schedule, have faith.

Remember the Law of Reverse Effort. If you harbor a fear of failure, the fear (subconscious mind) will overcome your will (conscious mind) to succeed.

ACTIVATE YOUR SUBCONSCIOUS MIND

Use emotions and images to energize your genie. Use words that evoke emotions and images. Avoid critical analysis and comparisons.

DETACH YOUR CONSCIOUS MIND

Thinking (conscious mind) of your affirmations hinders the genie. If you dwell on your affirmations consciously (in the beta state) you might think thoughts of failure. One hundred reasons might come to mind why you will fail. Practice detached acceptance.

GIVE THE JOB TO YOUR GENIE

Once you have programmed your subconscious mind, consciously let it go. Trust your genie. Give your affirmations to your genie and then forget about them. When you give a job to a faithful, competent employee, you trust him to do it. Micromanagement (conscious mind) only impedes the job. Do not micromanage your genie. Trust it. Do not tell your genie *how* to do the job.

USE EMOTION

Emotion is energy. Use emotions in your affirmations and when communicating with your genie. Ham it up. *Emote!*

SENSES

When giving your genie goals, use all of your senses. If you are programming for a new car, *see* the car, *smell* the new upholstery, *hear* the horn, *kick* the tires, *feel* the sensation of driving a new car.

GO INTO ALPHA

The alpha state is the door to the subconscious mind. Use it. Commands and affirmations will be accepted hundreds of times faster.

USE REPETITION

Feed your affirmation to your subconscious mind until it dominates. Feed it periodically to sustain it. Think of the "balance" symbol. Feed the positive side of the balance until it weighs more than the negative side and the positive side dominates.

USE IMAGINATION

Your subconscious mind does not know real from imagined. Use this to your advantage. Imagine yourself doing a skill correctly every time. Imagine yourself talking in front of a large audience with ease. Your delivery is lucid and given confidently. See the respect in the eyes of the audience. Imagine having a friendly, constructive conversation with the person with whom you argued at work. Imagine a different outcome. Imagine you sold a million dollars of real estate. Imagine you were promoted to your dream job.

REPLACE A BAD HABIT

You cannot change what is ingrained in your subconscious mind. But you can overpower it with its opposite. Feed the positive until it replaces the negative.

UPDATE YOUR GOALS

Go over your goals periodically. Your genie is seeking whatever it is fed. Feed it goals that will give you happiness, peace, and fulfillment.

MONITOR YOUR THOUGHTS

Your subconscious mind is a goal-seeking computer. *Always, always* feed it only positive, constructive, healthful

goals. Monitor what you say. Always! Every awake minute,
THINK OF YOURSELF ONLY AS YOU WANT TO BE.

INTRODUCTION

Most of the methods described here are easy and require little preparation. Do not be misled into thinking they are too easy to be effective, i.e., too easy to replace old habits or achieve success. Remember: you do not strain to use your subconscious mind. Straining is self-defeating. Using your subconscious mind has to be easy and effortless. Be glad that using your genie is easy.

These methods could be described using hundreds of words. I have used as few words as required, just enough to get the idea across. You have the background from the previous lessons to expand on the themes and add your personal touches to these methods. None of them are rigid. None must be followed exactly as described. Be imaginative. Personalize them. Use them. They work!

ADVERTISING

Before we get into the methods of using your genie, you need to know how ad men (and women) use the principles in the preceding lessons to influence *you*.

Advertising is a multi-billion-dollar industry. A minute during the Super Bowl alone costs millions of dollars. This money is not spent carelessly. Ad men know how to influence you.

There are six ways advertisers can get you to buy their products:

1. **Mechanical Force**—This is illegal and would cost too much.

2. **Drugs**—This is also illegal and impractical.

3. **Punishment**—This is illegal and hiring an army to punish people who refused to buy a product would not be cost effective.

4. **Reason**—I challenge you to name one product advertised on TV or in popular magazines that is based on reason. Reason is only used in the technical field. When an engineer needs a jaw crusher, for example, he looks in a catalog of jaw crushers and chooses one that fits his requirements. There is nothing emotional about the selection. But if a shampoo ad, for example, were based on reason it would be ineffective. Hundreds of brands are available and all of them do basically the same thing.

5. **Rewards**—This is a way of getting people to do what you want. Green Stamps used to be given with purchases. After enough were collected, they could be exchanged for merchandise. Some credit cards award a mile for every dollar you charge and when you amass 20,000 miles credit, it can be exchanged for an airline ticket. Rewards work but they are not the most efficient way of influencing you.

6. **Suggestion**—*Advertisers use suggestion.* Suggestion is an idea that one accepts uncritically and favorably, resulting in initiation of predictable behavior. *Suggestions are given to your subconscious mind, not your conscious mind!*

Each of the key principles discussed earlier is reviewed briefly to show how advertisers use them. Once you understand what advertisers are doing, you can control the influence ads have on you.

LOGIC

Advertisements are not logical because they are not aimed at your conscious mind. Suggestions are directed at your subconscious mind. Many, or most, of the products you buy are based on emotion, and emotion originates in the subconscious mind.

Now you understand why some advertisers have such dumb ads, like Jolly Green Giants and animated internal organs. They are planting suggestions in your subconscious mind, not your conscious mind. Is it logical to smoke cigarettes just because a macho cowboy does? Is it logical to wear a certain athletic shoe because Michael Jordan's name is on it? Is it logical to use a certain deodorant because it is fresh? Have you watched a TV ad and said to yourself, "This is so dumb?" It may be dumb to your conscious mind, but that is not where the ad is targeted.

ALPHA STATE

Suggestions are accepted much, much, more readily while you are in the alpha state. Years ago, Packard Vance stated in his book, *Hidden Persuaders*, that shoppers, particularly men, in grocery markets walked the aisles in the alpha state. While in the alpha state, they were particularly susceptible to buying on impulse.

Researchers have found that people watching TV are in the alpha state. TV is a highly proficient hypnotist. TV puts you in the alpha state and keeps you there. Most people just want to escape after a long day at work or school, relax, and turn off their minds (conscious minds). What do they do? They watch TV. Moreover, they often watch either mindless or emotional TV programs. This is a highly effective time for advertisers to plant suggestions in your subconscious mind.

You think that commercials are stupid, you hate them, and you pay no attention to them. Your conscious mind may tune commercials out but your subconscious mind, which is always alert, does not tune them out. The suggestion is more likely to be planted in your subconscious mind when your logical conscious mind is bored or distracted. TV is a perfect method for planting a suggestion in millions of unsuspecting people. It is so good that merchants spend billions of dollars to do it.

EMOTION

TV ads use emotion over logic. Many ads use fear as the motivator. Consider the image of a baby sitting in a tire, or a mother driving in a heavy rainstorm with a child sitting next to her. These advertisers use the fear of a possible accident to motivate you to buy their brand of tire. "Blonds have more fun." This is planting the fear of missing out on something if you are not a blond. If you do not buy their product, you may not have fun, be safe, have friends, etc.

TV ads are often placed at an emotional peak in TV programs. Just before a surprise witness is about to enter the courtroom, for example, the drama stops for a commercial. What a coincidence—a commercial just when you are most susceptible to suggestion.

IMAGINATION

If you drive a new sports car, you can imagine yourself feeling younger and doing things young people think of doing, like picking up babes. That is a good thought if you are young and single, but the ad is usually targeted more for middle-aged married men. Cigarettes, fortunately, are no longer advertised on TV. But remember the ads of sophisticated people smoking. Smoke and imagine that you too can be

sophisticated and attract friends. Now cigars are advertised on TV. A man smoking a cigar imagines that he is successful and important.

Think of the ads for Pepsi and Coke. They contain young, lively, active, energetic, happy people. Drink Pepsi and imagine yourself having the "good" life. Just by drinking Pepsi you will have good-looking, active, vivacious friends like the ones you see in the TV ads. You will have constant companionship and fun. And, how about the use of imagination in perfume ads? "There is a little of Eve in every woman." "All my men wear English leather, or they wear nothing at all."

An article on shampoos in a consumer magazine[1], opens with: "Shampoo merchants sell dreams. 'Use *Herbal Essence* and step into a garden of earthly delights, where every bubble smells of mysterious green herbs and freshly picked wild flowers. You'll feel alive with the clean of a mountain stream and the shine of the morning sun in your hair. And beautiful thoughts of far, faraway places in your head. Experience Clairol Herbal Essence shampoo…your hair will get very excited.' Shampoo merchants have to peddle dreams. How else can they get consumers to differentiate among the multitude of shampoos on the market?"

---

[1] *Consumer's Reports,* ca. 1975.

CONDITIONED REFLEX SUBSTITUTION

At the pretext of suggesting cures, ads actually suggest sicknesses. Before advertisers can promote their product, you must have some symptom their product can cure. Examples are:

- "It's coming...the flu season." Of course, that means you are going to get a headache, runny nose, etc.
- "When the flu strikes this year..." Everyone gets the flu, especially you!
- "The next time you get a headache..." Everyone gets headaches regularly.
- "Excedrin Headache number 34..." Getting headaches is natural and you should expect to get one. It is a status symbol.

A company can sell more aspirin by selling headaches. I read that aspirin manufacturers spend an excessive amount on advertising. It is hard to sell aspirin; it is easier to sell headaches.

The terrible thing about this is its influence on children. Children are even more susceptible to TV ads than adults. Children grow up to become part of our headache culture. They are led to believe that headaches are normal, everyone gets them, and whenever there is stress, a headache is inevitable.

At certain times of the year we are reminded that it is allergy season and we better be ready. We better have some of a specific medication on hand because we should *expect* that we will need it. We are bombarded with animated diagrams of pollen invading our sinuses and beautiful well-known personalities advising us to use a certain allergy medication.

IMAGES

Your subconscious mind communicates mostly with images rather than words. Advertisers use words to invoke images, as in the shampoo ad presented above. Images are particularly effective in TV ads. For example, there are animated cartoons, diagrams of a cut-away of a stomach depicting exaggerated heartburn, and driving a certain car into a cartoon paradise. In other words, drive this car and it will be like driving in paradise.

SYMBOLISM

Awhile back, Karl Malden made a lot of TV ads. Malden was effective because his image was a respected police lieutenant, a man of strength and in a powerful position. He always wore a hat. The hat was a symbol of authority. Catherine Deneuve and Elizabeth Taylor are symbols of glamour and sex. The Jolly Green giant is a symbol suggesting that if you eat these foods you will be strong, healthy, and happy. Cigars are the symbol of success and importance.

Robert Young, because of his TV roles in *Father Knows Best,* and as Marcus Welby, was a symbol of authority, integrity, and one who knew best. So if he said so, then it had to be true. If he said you could drink all the Sanka coffee you wanted, than it must be so.

REPETITION

Ads use of repetition to the point of nausea. Do ad men care that your conscious mind gets tired of the same old ad? Not at all. First, the ad is not aimed at your conscious mind and, second, when you get tired of it, you are more likely to consciously ignore it. When you consciously ignore it, the suggestion is more likely to be accepted by your subconscious mind.

INSTANT REPLAY

Some long ads, say 30 seconds, tell a story. After about a week, the ad is condensed to five seconds. The story is already wired in your subconscious mind. All the ad has to do is trigger your recollection of it. The advertiser has only to run a five-second ad and the entire 30-second ad plays in your subconscious mind. The advertiser just saved the cost of 25 seconds of airtime.

POLITICAL ADS

Political ads are not much different. Look for symbols of patriotism. The candidates in the last presidential campaign had a contest of who could get the most American flags in the background during their speeches. Are candidates logical? Unfortunately, not often. Emotion wins the most votes, not logic. Candidates cannot hold the attention of most voters long enough to present a thorough, logical analysis on any given topic. This is a quotation made by a political campaign consultant during a panel discussion: "You don't move people with words that are scholarly or judicious. You move people emotionally."

CONCLUSION

Now you know enough to defend yourself from being unduly influenced by advertisements. When the TV shows a sickly person blowing her nose, and the announcer says, "It's the flu season. . . ," replace that image with healthy thoughts and images.

WORRY

Worry incorporates most of the factors for planting a suggestion in your subconscious mind. The problem is that when you worry, you plant the suggestion in your subconscious mind of the thing you least want to happen! Your worry is your foremost thought and your foremost thought is the goal given to your subconscious mind. You are programming your subconscious mind for the thing you do not want. And that thought is emotional and repetitious! The thought keeps going around and around in your mind. And likely, it is exaggerated. Most worries are overblown.

Moreover, triggers constantly bring the worry to mind. For example, say your worry is losing your job and, consequently, your home, to which you are emotionally attached. Every time you think of your home, which is often, the thought acts as a trigger to rev up the worry emotion. Remember, your subconscious mind does not know real from imagined. So it is acting like the worst has happened. Your health will even be affected if the worry is allowed to persist.

Worry is a great way to program your mind if you want the worst for yourself. But you want the best, not the worst. Here are a couple of simple ways to allay worries.

PERFORM DIRECTED ACTIVITIES

Remember the Natural Energy Cycle in Chapter Four. The cycle is:

ENERGY ⟶ THOUGHT ⟶ EXPRESSION ⟶ REST ⟶ ENERGY ⟶ *etc.*

Worry breaks the cycle because it is expression by undirected activity. Undirected activity impedes complete

relaxation and, in addition, it is usually wasted time and energy. The emotional energy needs an outlet. If a dominant thought, such as a worry, is not expressed as directed activity, it is expressed as nail biting, fidgeting, etc. If the thought persists, it may be expressed as ulcers, high blood pressure, etc. So to maintain the Natural Cycle by using directed activity. Instead of worrying, do something constructive.

BRAINSTORM THE IMAGINED PROBLEM

Clearly define the problem and then think of as many solutions as you can. Do not reject any. After giving all solutions consideration, select the most sane and doable ones. Take action. Work on these solutions. For example, if you are worrying that you will lose your job; get your résumé up to date; discretely make inquiries about job openings at other companies; look into going back to school for an advanced degree. Use that emotional energy in a directed way. And when you have done all that you can, know just that: You have done all you can, so quit worrying.

Another important aspect of doing directed activities is that it gives you a feeling of being in control. A large part of the damage in worrying is the feeling of helplessness. Several studies in the health field have shown that patients who take an active roll in decision-making with their doctor do far better than those who let the doctor make the decisions unilaterally. When a patient participates, he feels like he has some control over the situation. When a patient does not actively participate with his doctor, he is more likely to feel helpless.

"I AM..."

"I am" is a powerful phrase. What you say after "I am" is an affirmation sent to your subconscious mind. Use these words wisely, because you use them dozens of times each day.

You use the "I am" phrase every time you exchange a greeting. Every time you pass a friend or colleague, they likely say, "How are you?" This is a friendly, customary greeting that most people use. What are typical responses?

- "I'm *fine.*" One meaning of "fine" is something of high quality, but it is an overused adjective and has a dubious meaning to your subconscious mind.

- "I'm okay." Just okay? Don't you want to be better than just okay?

- "I've been better." If you have been "better," then you are telling your subconscious mind that you are not very good now. Why leave your literal, emotional subconscious mind to interpret these banal responses?

When someone asks you how you are, use this as excuse to zap your subconscious mind with a positive affirmation. Respond with "I am...

- "Having a wonderful day."
- "Marvelous."
- "Wonderful."

It would be even better to say, "I am...

- "Healthy."
- "Successful."
- "Joyful and prosperous."
- "A beautiful person."
- "Intelligent and articulate."
- "A loving person."
- Etc.

Most of us do not have the audacity to say these affirmations aloud when someone asks how we are. That is

okay. You do not have to say them out loud; just shout them to yourself. Use these greetings as a reminder to feed positive affirmations to your subconscious mind.

Even if you do not adopt this suggestion, you must not respond with something you do not want to be. You do not want to be just "okay," just "fine," just "fair to middlin'," or just "better than some." You want the best for yourself. So affirm it!

The same is true for "I've got...," "I have...," and "I feel...." There are times when you may have a cold, but do not keep affirming it by repeating, "I've got a cold, my nose is stopped up, and I have a headache." .

There are times you have to describe your symptoms. For example, when you call your school or office to tell them you are sick, or when you are talking to your doctor. In these cases always preface your affirmation, even if it is only just to yourself, with "Until now...." This tells your subconscious mind that it has been a temporary condition and it is time to heal.

"IT WORKS!" *or I have been*

It Works is the title of a four- by six-inch, 25-page booklet. The author claims he could write 350 normal-sized pages on the subject but the gist can easily be described in only a few pages. The author claims he is well known (he only gives his initials, R.H.J) and he owes much of his success to the "It Works" method. This method does work and it is easy. Your genie does the work.

The method is this:

Step 1

Write down the things and conditions you want on three-inch by five-inch cards. Write each on a separate card.

Use the principles taught in this course. Be specific. Be descriptive. If you want money, write down how much you want. If you want a car, write down the make, model, and color. As you write this down, imagine yourself driving the car...smell the upholstery...kick the tires...and so on. Attach emotion to your words as you write them down. You even might sketch a picture of the thing you want.

Do not be timid. Do not hesitate to want too much. Amend your cards as necessary.

The author recommends a limit of three cards. Since the subconscious mind can do trillions of things at a time, this limit may be unnecessary. The number of cards you use is up to you.

Step 2

The author says to read the list early in the morning and late at night. He probably picked that up from Emile Couè. Whether the author, or Couè, knew it or not, they are telling you to read the cards while you are in the alpha state. Since you know how to go into the alpha state whenever you want, you can read your cards at times other than just on waking and falling asleep. Do not look at them while you are in the beta state. Your conscious mind will probably be critical and thoughts of failure may arise.

Step 3

Keep your desires to yourself. Sharing only dilutes the power in the subconscious mind and invites criticism and doubt. It also puts unnecessary pressure on you to succeed. Remember, any fear of failure will likely override the will to succeed.

Step 4

Do not tell your genie how to do it.

That's it. Simple but powerful. A large aerospace company where I worked bought an expensive program for their employees. The program was designed to help employees achieve goals. It was a good program with lessons, slides, tapes, etc. The presentations helped you analyze yourself and select suitable goals. But the bottom line was this:

Once you have determined what your goals are, write them on 3" x 5" cards, one goal per card. Read your cards first thing in the morning and last thing at night. Do not share them with anybody. Do not tell yourself how to accomplish your goals. Sound familiar?

Another man must have also made a fortune selling this method. About 25 years ago he ran full-page ads in major cities in the country. The title was *A Lazy Man's Way to Riches.* His spiel was mail order selling. But to achieve success he gave these instructions: Write your goals on 3" x 5" cards, one goal per card. Read your cards just after you wake up in the morning and just before you go to sleep. Do not share them with anybody. Do not tell your subconscious mind how to accomplish your goals.

It works! And it is easy!

PICTURED SUGGESTIONS

The purpose of this method is to repeatedly expose your subconscious mind to pictures of the things you want. After a short while your conscious mind will get bored and not pay attention to them, which is good. Every time the pictures come into view they will be noticed by your subconscious mind, which is great. These pictures act as icons in your subconscious mind computer and when activated, trigger your affirmation. This is all done on a subconscious level without interference from your conscious mind.

POSTER BOARD DISPLAY

This method requires a poster board, glue, and scads of old magazines. First, select your goals. Then thumb through the old magazines looking for good pictures of the things you want, or of things that remind you of what you want. For example, if you want a new house, select pictures of new houses. The pictures should be as close as possible to the house you want. Good pictures are colorful, descriptive, emotional, and active.

If you want to publish a book, look for pictures of books, libraries, and a list of the best-selling books. Write the title of your book on the best selling list with your name as author.

If you need a new car, cut out and paste pictures of the car you want on the poster board. Be as accurate as you can be. If you want a Volvo, use pictures of the Volvo you desire. A Volvo dealer would be a good source of pictures.

Display the poster board where only you will see it. You do not want friends asking questions about it. They might question your ability to own a Volvo and plant the seed of doubt. Remember: do not think about how to do it, or how to get it. That is the job of your genie.

DREAM BOOK

Phyllis Diller described her "dream book" in an interview that appeared in a newspaper years ago. She said, "Everyone should own a dream book. I have one and it's part of the reason I've been so successful." Her dream book—which she never let anyone see—was filled with her hopes and dreams, most of which came true. "I started it years ago when I dreamed of becoming a star. If there was something I wanted, no matter how ridiculous or impossible, I wrote it down or drew a picture in the book."

A dream book has an advantage over a poster because it is easier to keep private. It is not easy to hide a large poster but it is easy to conceal a scrapbook from friends, and even from your spouse or parent. Diller just wrote and drew pictures, but why not spice yours up with colored pictures from magazines too?

CONDITIONING EXERCISE—CLEAR

Personal computer users clean up their hard drives regularly. During normal operation, files tend to get fragmented and parts of unwanted files get separated and left behind. These fragmented and unwanted files interfere with the operation of the computer. They are counterproductive. Programs are built into Windows to help clean up file fragments and clear out programs that are potentially harmful.

You need to do the same thing with your subconscious mind's hard disk. There are programs from childhood that are harmful. There are programs from adulthood that are counterproductive and affect your physical and mental health. These programs include jealousies, vengefulness, loss of temper, grudges, etc.

You are aware of some of these programs. The ones you are aware of can be dealt with. Correct the situation with directed activity. Call the person you are angry with, for example, and work it out. If you cannot bring yourself to actually talk to the person, you can do it in your imagination in alpha. Your subconscious mind does not know the difference between reality and vivid imagination. Go into alpha and work it out constructively with the person.

Most of the harmful programs in our subconscious mind were acquired in childhood and we are unaware they even exist. Some were acquired in adulthood and, because of the

emotion attached to them, are buried in our subconscious minds. These negative programs can seriously affect your physical and emotional health. They need to be cleared. Actually, you know that programs cannot be erased from your subconscious mind but you can override them with positive ones. That is the purpose of this affirmation.[2]

"CLEAR " ROUTINE

Get comfortable. If you are sitting, put your feet flat on the floor and lay your hands comfortably on your lap. Raise your eyes up 20 degrees. Looking up is a strain on your eyelids. Your eyelids are getting tired. Your eyelids are tired and they begin to flutter. You now want to close your eyes. Try to keep them open, but you cannot. The harder you try to keep them open, the more they want to close. Allow your eyelids to close. Your eyes are closed.

Imagine you are a life-size weather balloon. Someone has over-filled you with air. You can feel the tension and you want to relax. There is an exhaust valve by your hand. Open it and relieve the pressure. Let all of the air drain out until the balloon is lying flat on the ground. Be aware that it is devoid of tension. It is completely relaxed. All tension has escaped.

Breathe slowly and deeply. Let yourself relax. Relaxation is the easiest thing you can do. Simply let go...just let go. Let your mind drift on pleasant thoughts...peaceful thoughts...happy thoughts. You are safe and secure.

Just let your body relax...completely relax...from head to foot. Search for remnants of tension in your body and then visualize them draining from your body. See these vestiges of tension flowing out of your body and draining harmlessly on the floor. You are relaxed. Every muscle in your body is relaxed...limp...soooo relaxed. You are feeling heavy now. Heavier

---

[2] A CD that includes this routine can be purchased at www.TheGenieWithin.net. For more information contact TheGenieWithin@roadrunner.com or write to *The Genie Within,* 1844 Fuerte Street, Fallbrook, CA 92028.

and heavier. You are going deeper and deeper into a healthy, natural state of relaxation and peace of mind. You don't even have to listen to my voice...just relax. Relax and let go. See yourself as that deflated balloon...totally limp...totally relaxed.

Imagine that you are entering an elevator. It is a very safe elevator—well built and well designed. The walls are soft and the lighting is a subdued bluish color. You notice there is an operator...and the operator looks familiar to you. You realize that the operator is your subconscious mind. Your operator knows where you are going. Your operator closes the door and you begin to go down...down. Your operator is taking you to a healthy, deep state of mind...a state where your subconscious mind is open to healthful, positive suggestions...where it only accepts suggestions for your highest good.

Feel the lightness in your body as you descend. You are descending deeper and deeper. You notice that there are 10 floors...and you just passed number 10. The elevator continues descending...safely...steadily. Feel the lightness of your body due to the decent of the elevator. Now you notice that you passed floor 9...and you continue down...downward. And as you descend, you go deeper and deeper asleep...deeper and deeper asleep. The light in the cab grows dimmer and dimmer. The elevator cab grows darker and darker. You are now passing floor 8...now floor 7. You are now in a deep healthy state of mind...deeper then you have been before. It is pleasant...it is peaceful...it is calm and wonderful. Floors 6, 5, and 4. You are going to an even deeper level of mind...deeper and deeper. Floors 3 and 2 pass by. You are now at floor 1.

You are now at the deepest level of sleep...you are at a level where you can easily program your subconscious mind with healthy and loving and positive affirmations. Your subconscious mind eagerly accepts all healthful, positive suggestions. Your subconscious mind is happy to comply with the requests from your conscious mind. Your subconscious mind lovingly works with your conscious mind for your best interests, and best health. Your subconscious mind eagerly accepts the positive affirmations from your conscious mind.

The elevator has stopped and your subconscious mind opens the door. The scene you see is gorgeous...beautiful beyond words. It is a meadow...and the meadow is filled with thousands of wild flowers...of all colors...of all sizes. There are tame animals...deer...foxes...squirrels. All are friendly and harmless. They do not mind your presence. You all seem to be part of the scene...part of nature. You feel like you belong there. You are glad to be there.

You find that you do not need a path to walk on...you seem to float over the flowers. You are weightless...you are free...you are ecstatic...you are in paradise. Now rest under a shady tree and accept the following affirmations as yours for now and for always...for your good...for your best health...for your best mental being.

Each and every time you want to return to this relaxed, healthy state of mind, count down 3 - 2 - 1 and mentally say and think the word "RELAX." Each and every time you wish to return to this deep state of mind simply count down and think and mentally say the word "RELAX." Each time you do this you return to this state faster and easier...faster...easier. Using the word "relax" in normal conversation has no effect on you. Only when you intend to go into this state does it have this effect.

Ordinary sounds act only to deepen your sleep. In any emergency you are naturally wide awake instantly, alert and aware of your surroundings.

Now accept this following affirmation as yours. Let it sink deep into your subconscious mind for your highest good. Imagine you are saying the following words to yourself.

I accept myself as I am. I am what I am now because of my past experiences. All of these past experiences have had value in some way that was not evident to me then. I accept my past...all of it...as a valuable learning experience. Whatever happened in the past happened for a reason and I am better today for it. I am glad for everything that has happened to me. All experiences that seemed unnecessary at the time or seemed hurtful have steeled me...strengthened me...toughened me...made me more compassionate...made me more understanding...made me more

appreciative of myself and of life...made me a better person. I look at these experiences with a positive point of view. I accept each experience for what it was, a learning experience. I visualize a beautiful diamond and realize that it is beautiful and precious and rare because it has been formed by severe pressure and heat. It has used these adverse conditions to become something beautiful and precious.

Right now is the only moment I can live...and I choose to live it fully and joyfully. Today I am alive and I rejoice. Today I love life...I love myself...I love everyone I come in contact with. I find some truth and beauty in every person I meet. I dwell on their positive attributes. Life is good to me. I accept my good and I am very thankful...ever so thankful. And I wish this good for all mankind too. The universe is abundant and can provide for everyone.

Today I release the effect of every negative experience of the past and every negative effect it had on me. I love myself for what I am and I extend this feeling to everyone else. I wish for everyone to have all the good they deserve. I want all the good there is for myself and for everybody. I know that we all share this planet, and we are all a part of Life. I accept everyone as I accept myself.

I act and do what I think is right at that time. Sometimes I may look back and wish I had acted differently. But it is useless to wish I did something differently. I live in the NOW. I only look back when it is of help to me now. I now forgive myself for every mistake I have ever made; and I forgive everyone who has in any way harmed me, because in every experience, as I understand it, good surely comes to me in some way. Each mistake I have made has led to greater understanding and to greater opportunity. I am thankful for every experience of the past. I can release...I do release...I release my resistances to releasing. I now fully release what I thought were mistakes and release their effect on me. I feel much better without the effect they had on me. I completely forgive myself. I completely forgive others who I thought harmed me. They thought they were doing the right thing at that time. Their action taught me a lesson and strengthened me in some way.

I look forward to tomorrow but I live in the now. I am ever aware of myself and my surroundings because I live in the now. I am grateful for my new level of understanding. I now agree with Life. I am born anew. I now eagerly look forward to living every moment. I am aware of every moment...I appreciate every moment.

I now see myself standing in front of a large window. It is difficult to see the meadow, the flowers, and the animals on the other side because the window is dirty. It is covered with years of dirt...negative thoughts...hurts...bad thoughts...slurs...vengeful thoughts...envy...etc.

There is a large sponge and squeegee on a long handle. There is also a bucket of soapy water. I see myself dipping the sponge in the soapy water and washing all the dirt and grime off the window. When it is clean, I see myself taking the squeegee and drying the window. Now I can see through the window clearly. The meadow is crystal clear...the whole world is now clear and beautiful...the world is clean...pure...lovely...loving. I love life and all that lives. All life loves me. I see clearly now. I am free of the effect of past negative experiences. My subconscious mind is free of the effect of all counterproductive programs. My subconscious mind is free to dwell only on the positive...only on healthy thoughts...only on loving thoughts...to live now, in the present. I feel lighter...I feel joy...I feel optimistic.

Now it is time to return to the awake state...to return to full awareness. I return to the elevator and enter it. The operator closes the door and I begin to ascend...1...2...I am waking up...I am returning to the awake state with a renewed outlook...with a totally positive attitude...with a loving attitude toward myself and everyone else. It shows and others sense it. 3...I feel wonderful...I feel lighter...I feel as if a burden has been taken off my shoulders...I feel free...I feel loving...4...5...6...I am refreshed...7...I feel joyful...8...I see clearly the beauty of life...feeling refreshed...9 and 10! I am wide awake!

METHODS of Using Your Subconscious Mind, Part 2

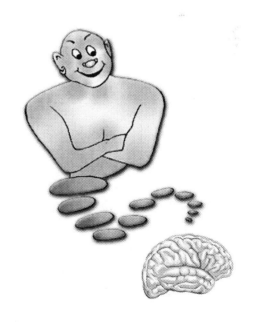

Lesson Seven

Methods of Using Your Subconscious Mind, Part 2

TURN ON YOUR "JOY" CENTER

F eeling blue? Want to feel happy? Stimulate your "Joy" center.[1]

Fifty years ago, Dr. Robert Heath, a neurologist and psychiatrist at Tulane University School of Medicine, electrically stimulated the septum pellucidum area in the brain of patients suffering from severe depression. The electrical stimulation immediately altered the patients' moods from severe depression to joyfulness.

Dr. Heath attached wires to the area, brought the wires out of the patient's heads, and attached the wires to a battery. This allowed his patients to activate the septum pellucidum by pressing a button. Now, when they became depressed, they pressed the button, their septum pellucid was stimulated, and their mood changed from depression to happiness. The problem was that the thin wires often detached or broke. Besides, wires coming out of someone's head are not practical (or attractive). Thus, this way of altering mood was not

---

[1] *"Access Your Brain's Joy Center,"* by Pete A. Sanders Jr., Free Soul Publishing, Sedona, AZ

accepted. The idea of stimulating this area in the brain was, however, picked up by pharmaceutical companies. These companies developed drugs to alter patients' moods, often with undesirable side effects.

Stimulating your septum pellucidum mentally is better than using drugs and it is without side effects. First you need to know where your septum pellucidum is located. Picture a horizontal line going into your head just above the bridge of your nose. This spot is often called the "third eye." Then picture a horizontal line going in from just above your left ear. The septum pellucidum area is where the lines meet. The septum pellucidum is fibrous and delicate.

Stimulate the septum pellucidum like this. Relax and go into the alpha state. Tell your subconscious mind you want to stimulate your septum pellucidum to make you feel happy and joyful. Your subconscious mind knows where it is. Act as if it does and be confident that you are going to become happy and joyous. Mentally  picture the fibrous area in your brain as a delicate string instrument and very gently strum it barely touching the strings. It is that easy. Here is a suggested conditioning routine.

CONDITIONING EXERCISE— JOY CENTER

"JOY CENTER" ROUTINE

Close your eyes. Allow yourself to relax...deeply relax.

Let go of all tension. Be aware of your head and let it relax. The muscles in your head are now relaxed. Be aware of your shoulders and arms. The muscles in your shoulders and arms are now relaxed. Be aware of your torso. The muscles in your back, chest, and stomach are now relaxed. Be aware of your buttocks and legs. The muscles in your buttocks and legs are now relaxed.

Now relax your mind. Count...3...2...1...and picture the word "ALPHA." You are now in the healthy alpha state of consciousness. Your subconscious mind is open and eager to obey your positive, healthful suggestions.

Go even deeper into the alpha state. I am going to count from 10 to 1. When I get to 1, you are in the deepest alpha. 10...9...8...7...6...5...4...3...2...1. You are now at an even deeper level.

Think of a time you were very happy. Picture your reactions. See the big smile on your face. Hear yourself react to the feelings of happiness. Hear your laughter. Feel the warmth, goodness, and tingling throughout your body. Enjoy this feeling...relish it..retain it.

You now have the intent to stimulate your septum pellucidum, your joy center, and you expect to make yourself even happier.

Visualize your brain and, in your mind's eye, enter your brain on your left side just above your left ear. Proceed to the center of your brain where your joy center is located. Your subconscious mind knows where it is.

Picture your joy center as a tiny delicate angel's harp. Now gently...ever so gently...strum the strings of the harp. And as you strum the thin strings of the harp, feel the vibrations...feel happier and happier. Once again gently strum the strings and instantly feel the warm glow of happiness engulf you. The happiness starts

in your limbic system and sends neurotransmitters throughout your body. Everywhere. Even your hands feel happy...joyful...your feet and legs feel happy. Your entire body feels joy and happiness. Relish this feeling and remember it.

Feel a large happy grin form on your face. The source is from your limbic system. You cannot stop the grin. Go ahead and try. The harder you try, the bigger your grin gets. That's okay. Go ahead and smile...you're happy.

Any time you want to feel happy and joyful...any time you want to feel positive and upbeat, simply go into the alpha state and gently strum your joy center harp. Your harp loves to be played. It only takes a few strums. It's very effective. Your subconscious mind loves to feel happy and joyful. Your body loves to be happy. Feelings of happiness stimulate your immune system. Feelings of happiness promote good health. Feelings of happiness promote an upbeat, delightful sense of humor. Feelings of happiness make you even more lovable. Feelings of happiness make you capable of loving even more than you do now.

Remember your joy center. Your joy center can reverse any negative mood. Your joy center can learn to be active all the time. Let it be active. Encourage it. Allow your joy center harp to play the tune of happiness all the time. Allow your immune system to be active and happy, all the time. Allow your body...all of it...all your organs...all your muscles...all your joints...all of your neural system...your blood...everything about you...every cell in your body to feel and express happiness. Exude happiness.

Now return to the awake state and bring all of these happiness feelings with you. They are yours...yours to keep...yours to use for your highest good.

3...2...1...wide awake and happy!

SUBCONSCIOUS CROCK-POT

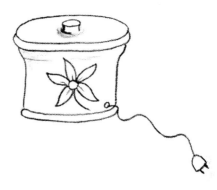

Crock-pots cook meals while the cook is away doing something else. Crock-pots cook slowly at a low temperature. Your subconscious mind is "cooking" 24 hours a day and it can do trillions of things simultaneously. So ,why not allow your genie to work for you while you do other things, even while you sleep?

Rev. Eric Butterworth is a successful Unity minister in New York City who has a reputation for "impromptu" sermons. Well, they are not exactly impromptu. This is the way he describes his method of preparing sermons.

One month before he delivers the sermon he writes the subject on the tab of a folder. He jots down all the thoughts he has on a sheet of paper and tucks it in the folder. He puts the folder in a special drawer and then forgets it (consciously.) One month later, the sermon is formulated in his mind with little conscious effort.

What Rev. Butterworth really does is put the sermon in his subconscious crock-pot. He gives his subconscious crock-pot the goal of preparing the sermon for him. Then, he "forgets" it consciously, but his subconscious mind picks up ideas, organizes, and stores them in his *mental* folder.

Let's say the subject of the sermon is "Love." During the next week, someone in his congregation tells him a story that epitomizes unselfish love expressed by a benevolent act. The story is unconsciously filed in his mental folder. Later Rev. Butterworth reads a heart-warming story about the devotion

expressed by an elderly couple. This story is also unconsciously filed in his mental folder. His subconscious mind is also organizing the sermon so when the Sunday arrives, Rev. Butterworth seems to talk off the cuff, but actually the sermon has been incubating for a month.

I used this method successfully in my career in aerospace. Due to the nature of aerospace work, there was seldom time to write reports ahead of time. We were so busy daily doing hot jobs that those monthly, quarterly, and semiannual reports snuck up on us, leaving inadequate time to prepare them.

I solved this problem by giving the job to my mental crock-pot. Well ahead of the due date of a given report, I would do my best to outline the report and jot down all my ideas. This only took a few minutes. Usually the content of the proposed report would be unorganized. I just wrote down whatever I could in no particular order.

During the time when my subconscious crock-pot was cooking, thoughts would bubble up from my subconscious mind. For example, I might realize that another chemical analysis was needed to prove a critical point, or that I needed to send away for some necessary information. Then, when I started to write the report at the last minute, the information was available and the outline was already organized in my mind. Many times the report flowed with little effort. Had I not started the report early in my subconscious crock-pot, I would have been up most of the night before it was due, and the hurried report would not have been as complete or coherent.

Here is another example of how I used my subconscious crock-pot. I decided that I wanted to supplement my income. I programmed my genie to come up with ideas for new products my wife and I could make and sell.

The first idea came unexpectedly on a ski trip. Skiers were still using heavy, bulky boot trees to carry their ski boots.

Those boot trees were designed to keep the old wooden boot bottoms flat while they dried. Boots were now made of plastic and did not warp. Boot trees were no longer needed.

One day I looked at the old boot tree and an idea popped into my head. All that was needed was just two straps. One horizontal strap held the boots together while a vertical strap kept the boots from slipping out of the horizontal strap and provided a carrying handle. This carrier was simple, inexpensive, durable, and much easier to store when not in use. The idea was successful—too successful. My wife and I were selling small quantities, when a distributor ordered 10,000 units to start with. My wife and I realized we did not have the time to manage a small business that could handle subcontracts, shipping, and record keeping.

Another idea came to me one day while shopping. I rode a bicycle to work at the time and I was using one of those postage-stamp-size rear view mirrors that attached to your eyeglasses or cap. The small field of vision was inconvenient and actually dangerous. You had to maneuver your head to position the mirror. Maneuvering your head and concentrating on this small mirror while riding a bicycle is unsafe.

While in a Pic-N-Save store, I happened to notice a pocket, wide-angle, lightweight mirror intended for a woman's purse. Normally I would have paid no attention to a lady's mirror but at the time my subconscious mind was programmed to look for ideas. The idea came to me instantly. I bought a dozen of the mirrors, took them home, and designed a bicycle mirror that attached to my wrist. I could observe the area from my knee to the curb on the other side of the street without having to maneuver the mirror. It made a perfect bicycle mirror.

After about a month I had to unplug my subconscious crock-pot. I had filled several pages in a notebook with ideas. Many ideas had potential, but I just did not have the time or the inclination to become a part-time businessman.

Bill Lear epitomized the merit of the subconscious crock-pot. He learned about this method from *The Power of Universal Mind,* by Robert Collier. The method for achieving success in the book had three simple steps: 1) provide your subconscious mind with all the information available on the problem, 2) ask your subconscious mind to come up with solutions and, 3) simply forget about it. Go off and do something else, preferably something relaxing. In 21 days, solutions to your problem will spill out of your mind.

Using this method, Bill Lear, with only an eighth-grade education, invented a tuning coil for car radios and made his first million dollars before he was 21 years old. Lear probably did not know that a college professor declared in a scientific paper that tuning coils could not be made small enough for use in automobiles. Using his subconscious mind he went on to invent the:

- 8-track cassette
- Dynamic speaker
- Autopilot
- Direction finder
- Radio transceiver

Plus, he had 148 other patents.

After a giant aerospace company told the government it would take an experienced aeronautical design team 10 years and $100 million to design a small business jet, Bill Lear and his small staff designed it and had it certified in two years for $10 million. Sales were $52 million in the first year.

You have a genie that can solve problems for you too. Using your subconscious crock-pot is energy and time efficient and costs nothing.

GUIDED IMAGERY

Guided imagery is powerful. It can be used by itself and it can be, and generally is, integrated with other methods of using your genie.

Guided imagery can be used for achieving almost anything, for example, getting high grades in school, healing the body, modifying habits and personality traits, achieving goals, and for improving physical skills.

Guided imagery is used universally in sports. It is a standard part of training at Olympic camps. Many famous athletes used visualization even before it became popular. Baseball pitchers visualize where they want the ball to go over the plate before they throw it; golfers visualize their swing and the flight of the ball before each swing, and; basketball players visualize their shots swishing through the basket each time and what their response is when the man they are guarding makes certain moves.

Slalom skiers often cannot make practice runs on the course because practice runs produce ruts that ruin the course. So they walk beside the course and memorize it. Then they sit down, relax, and visualize skiing down the course. They rehearse each turn. If you were to watch the daydreaming skier, you would see her muscles twitch as she makes each turn down the course.

Stephen Simonton and Stephanie Matthews-Simonton pioneered the use of visualization in helping advanced cancer patients. The Simontons relaxed their patients (i.e., put them into the alpha state) and had them visualize their bodies fighting the cancer. Each patient would be asked to personalize his or her approach. For example, a housewife might picture going into the cancerous area and vacuuming the diseased cells with a super powerful vacuum cleaner. A vacuum cleaner would be meaningful to her. A policeman might go into the

diseased area and shoot the cancer cells with his pistol. A military man might go in with tanks and flamethrowers. The best for you is what *feels* best for you. What feels best comes from the subconscious mind. Let your subconscious mind select your visual props.

One of the Simonton's first patients was 67 years old and had a grave case of throat cancer. He went from 130 to 98 pounds. He could barely swallow and had difficulty breathing. He was given a 5% chance of living five years. The Simontons had him use imagery for about ten minutes, three times each day. He also went through the standard radiology treatment. He visualized the radiation as millions of bullets. He imagined the cancer cells getting weaker and giving up. He imagined his normal cells getting stronger and resisting the bullets. He also visualized his white cells swarming and overcoming the cancer cells.

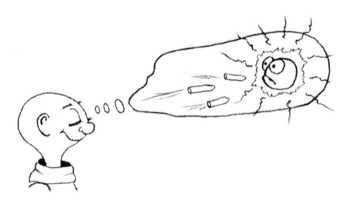

The cancer disappeared in two months. Would the cancer have been cured without the imagery? That cannot be proven, but those involved with the case did not think so. Encouraged by his success with cancer, the patient then cured his arthritis, exclusively with imagery.

There are several books on guided imagery but they only tend to complicate it. The method is simple: go into the alpha state and visualize the desired result. And, of course, use all of the basics you learned in the first four lessons, namely, emotion, repetition, expectation of success, a positive attitude, and use all of your senses. And, after your visualization session, thank your subconscious mind and then let go. Do not think about it in the beta state because your conscious mind may plant seeds of doubt.

Early in my engineering career, I was asked to defend an original experimental approach I was using for a critical part of a nuclear fuel project. My problem was two-fold. One, I was out of school only a few years and I had the audacity to break from tradition and use a new experimental approach. Two, I was petrified of public speaking and I would have to make my presentation in front of 40 skeptical, competitive scientists. I prepared my talk and practiced it in the alpha state. I visualized the audience smiling and looking at me in a friendly, compassionate way. I knew that they understood my approach and could see its advantages. I even pictured them clapping after I was finished. When I gave my talk I was confident, relaxed, and being relaxed, I was able to think clearly. The talk went well and the Department Director wrote a letter for my personnel file that commended me on an excellent presentation. He also said that it was the first presentation in our department in which the audience clapped. I have been comfortable talking to audiences since.

Let your subconscious mind guide you in selecting images. It knows what motivates it better than you do. Also, use all your senses during your visualizations to invoke as much emotion as you can. If you have trouble thinking up a good image you might look through magazines for vivid, active, colorful photographs. I have a two-page picture from *Life* magazine of a small tugboat guiding a gigantic ocean liner

into port. This is my image of my conscious mind leading my subconscious mind—me leading my genie. Another is a two-page photo of the bright red afternoon sun. This, to me, represents the power in my subconscious mind.

The possibilities of using imagery are endless. Use it!

CHILDREN

Children are highly susceptible to programming. So, use this to their (and your) advantage. In Lesson No. 2, you learned that a newborn baby has an empty hard drive (the mammalian part of the subconscious mind) that soaks up new programs. Parents must keep this in mind constantly. Children should be allowed and encouraged to experience new things. They should be exposed to a variety of colors, activities, sounds, vocabulary, and music. And they should be fed positive, confidence-building affirmations.

Not only should children be exposed to the outside world but they must be nurtured verbally. You were taught in these lessons to only think of yourself as you want yourself to be. This reasoning must be applied to children. *Tell children only what you want them to become.* Feed them positive affirmations at every opportunity, and *never* feed them negative ones.

Never say things like, "Don't be so clumsy," "Can't you do it right?" or "You just don't learn, do you?" These affirmations, if repeated or said with a lot of emotion, will become programs in their subconscious minds. Even comments in jest, if said repeatedly and with emotion, will have impact. Consider such comments as "you are going to grow up to be a *big* girl," "You are such a *naughty* boy," or "You are such a *silly* girl."

Two techniques work well on children. The first is to tell the child short stories with lots of positive affirmations and a good moral as they are falling asleep. The validity of sleep-

learning is arguable but, nonetheless, I recorded stories and played the tapes at low volume as my children were falling asleep and even after they had fallen asleep.

Make up the stories: it is easy. Stories that you make up are more personal and tailored to the child. An example might be a story of a happy loving family eating a peaceful meal together. Everyone is pleasant and has an opportunity to talk about what they did or felt that day. Everyone uses good manners and speaks distinctly and clearly. The children sense that the parents love them and this gives them a true sense of confidence and poise.

Another story might be how everyone has talents. And this child develops his or hers, whatever it is. Being able to do something better than most people gives them confidence and pride. They can see the value in this so they work at it more efficiently and practice longer to develop these talents.

The second method is to play some music they enjoy or read an entertaining story to them. The music or story is fed into the right ear where it is neurologically carried to the left half of the brain. In the right-brain-left-brain model, the left side is the logical, rational brain, the characteristics of the conscious mind.

While the logical side of the brain is engrossed in the music or story, quietly read affirmations in the left ear. These affirmations will be carried to the right side of the brain. The right side is associated with feelings and global thinking, characteristics of the subconscious mind. Thus the affirmation bypasses the critical mind and goes directly to the uncritical, subconscious mind.

ONE-WORD AFFIRMATIONS

Words have two meanings. One is the definition found in dictionaries. Words also have connotations attached to them. These connotations are beyond the logical definition and are associated with our personal feelings. For example, the definition of "flag" is a piece of cloth that represents a country, etc. But when we think of the word "flag" many thoughts, emotions, and images come into consciousness from the subconscious mind.

These connotations and images can be used to our advantage as one-word affirmations.

"TRY"

The connotation of "try" is to attempt to do something but not do it. Try to pick up something within reach, say a pencil. Did you pick it up? If you did, you did not "try" to pick it up. When you "try" to pick it up, you fail to pick it up. Thus, the word means, to the subconscious mind, "to fail!"

Now that you know the connotations in this word, why would you ever use it? Do not use it! When you ask Sally if she will come to church at six a.m. to help set up decorations for a special event and she says, "I'll *try* to be there," she will not be there. If you ask Shirley and she says, "I'll be there," you can count on her.

Eliminate this insidious word from your vocabulary. First, it is self-defeating and, second, there is always a better word. Why *try* to do something? Just *do* it. Why try to hammer a nail? Hammer a nail. Why try to read the book? Read the book. Why try to get into college? Study hard and get into college. Why try to be a better person? Be a better person.

There are two exceptions. One is in writing. Clear, easy-to-read writing requires the use of simple, short words and

"try" fits both requirements. The use of the synonyms, "attempt," "strive" and "endeavor," are not as pithy. So use it in writing if you must, but not in conversation.

Two, another definition of "try" is "to test." This is a legitimate use. But considering the dozens of times you use the word "try" every day, very few, if any, are used to mean, "to test." So rather than use the word "try" for this legitimate use, use another, better word that is more precise. Don't "try" a piece of pie; "taste" a piece. Don't "try" another newspaper; "read" another one. Don't "try" another car; "drive" another car.

"DELETE"

When a TV ad for a cold remedy comes on and the announcer says "When you catch your next cold...," immediately think the word "DELETE." When someone says, "You do not look well," immediately picture "DELETE." Picture yourself at your computer. Visualize the negative statement on your monitor screen. Highlight it and "DELETE" it. These are suggestions you do not want impacting your subconscious mind. The word "DELETE" is a command to your subconscious mind to ignore what was just said or seen.

"CANCEL"

Use this word the same as above. Add power to this word by imagining a big neon sign flashing the word "CANCEL" in vivid colors.

"DONE"

Everyone at times has a task that seems too big. Have you ever arrived at work and found your desk piled with papers that need immediate attention? Or come home from school with several big assignments that had to be done that night? Most people give themselves self-defeating affirmations like, "How will I ever get all of this done?" Or, "I can't do all of this!"

Instead, picture the word "DONE." A good affirmation depicts the thing you want in the present time. The thing you want is for the work to be "DONE." You know it will be "DONE" if you simply get busy and do it rather than feel sorry for yourself. Whenever you feel you have too much work, simply picture the work "DONE." Then add power to the one-word affirmation by seeing yourself dancing on a clean desk or seeing yourself handing your completed assignments to your teachers.

"GOING"

Emile Coué reported much success on patients with pain. He had them say, "It is GOING" ten times as rapidly as they could. Cleverly, he reasoned that when the patient said the short sentence as fast as they could, the conscious mind had to think about the *saying*, not the meaning. Thus, the suggestion of "GOING" went into the subconscious mind.

"GONE"

Use for any malady, such as a cold or a wart.

"CHANGE"

When you are worried about something, or have a negative thought running around in your head, think

"CHANGE." Think "CHANGE" and then think about something else. You can only think of one thing at a time so you have a choice of what to think about. Change your thought and exercise your ability to think of something positive. Think of something happy and something that will keep your attention, like reliving a special vacation.

"NUMB"

When you slam your finger in the car door, your reaction is to think and say "ouch." "Ouch" connotes pain and pain is not what you want. Instead, get in the habit of reacting with the word "NUMB."

"NORMAL"

After you slam your finger in the car door, your body reacts by sending fluids to that area that cause swelling. Often the swelling does more damage than the smashing, so use these words together, "NUMB and NORMAL!"

"DRY"

If you feel the sniffles coming on. Think "DRY and NORMAL." Associate "DRY" with something vivid. Recall the opening scene in the movie, *The English Patient.* The hero was flying low over the vast Sahara desert. No vegetation was visible from horizon to horizon, only sand. That is DRY.

"REACH"

Need to be creative? Think "REACH." Imagine "REACHING" for ideas out of thin air and inserting them inside your head.

SUMMARY

Many other words can be used as one-word affirmations. A word will be especially powerful for you if you provide connotations to it. For example, you want your conscious mind and subconscious mind to work together. Think "TOGETHER" and imagine two people hugging, a two-person volleyball team showing teamwork skills, or two lumberjacks working one of those old two-man saws. Now every time you think of "TOGETHER," you activate and strengthen the affirmation and remind your conscious mind and subconscious mind to work "TOGETHER."

PARABLES

To add even more power to your one-word affirmation, make up a parable to go with it. Parables impress your subconscious mind better than merely words or static images. They supply wisdom and energy at a subliminal level. Writers and storytellers have used parables for ages because of their impact. Once you hear a meaningful parable, you never forget it.

An example of a parable to use with the one-word affirmation "TOGETHER" is given below.

"A farmer owned a hundred oxen but the oxen would not plow his fields no matter how much he beat them with a whip. One day the farmer found that one of the oxen could talk. The ox told him the oxen would not work for the farmer because he gave them confusing orders, abused them, and did not credit them for their effort. The farmer became wise and compassionate. He gathered the oxen together in the field. He

explained that if they worked "TOGETHER" with him, he would thank them profusely, he would share the harvest with them, and he would house them in a barn during the long, cold winter. He added that plowing would be effortless if the oxen followed directions and worked "TOGETHER." Combined they were much more powerful than when alone. The oxen complied and farmer and the oxen prospered."

Now when you think of "TOGETHER" it will impress your subconscious mind even more. Making up your own parable will mean more to your subconscious mind than one made up by someone else.

Here is an example of a parable for getting rid of the excess baggage, such as grudges, envy, regrets, unfulfilled desires, poor decisions, etc.

"An elderly man with a gaunt, troubled face was walking through a village. He drew a lot of attention from the villagers because he was carrying so many objects with him. One little boy, who did not know it was impolite to ask, stopped the man and asked him why he had an iron stove on his back. "Oh, that" said the man. "I really do not need that for where I am going and it is very heavy. I will leave it here." The man walked a little farther when an old lady asked him if he really needed the cast iron curling iron he had attached to his belt. "No, I do not need that. I did not know it was there," he replied. He gladly gave her the curling iron. A little later, a younger man approached and asked if he would sell the iron anvil he was balancing on his head. "I was so used to carrying

that anvil that I forgot it was there," the old man said. "You may have it for I am glad to rid myself of it." The old man went through the village unburdening himself of all that was unnecessary and only caused him grief. By the time he walked through the village he was free of all his burdens. He was enormously grateful to those who helped him realize he was carrying things that made his life harder and that were unhealthy. His pace increased and he smiled broader than he had for years. He whistled all the way home, where he lived many, many more years, and had a happy, fulfilling, and healthy life."

SUBSTITUTION

"Always think of yourself as you want yourself to be." Most of the time thinking positively is easy. But there are times when you may have a problem or ailment that you keep thinking about. Remember you can only think of one thing at a time and your conscious mind has free will. So you have a choice of what you think about. Here are a few ideas to use when you are having trouble keeping your conscious mind off negative thoughts.

First, do all directed activity items you can think of. Do not break the Natural Cycle: Energy —>Idea —>Directed Activity—>Rest —>Energy —>etc. Doing something positive helps in two ways. You burn energy in a constructive way instead of suppressing it, and doing something positive gives you a feeling of being in control.

Second, every time your conscious mind turns to the negative thought, substitute it:

- Picture a positive "One-Word" affirmation.
- Visualize a symbol, such as a happy face.
- Envision a pleasant scene, possibly a place where you had a happy time.
- Chant a positive phrase, such as "I am happy" or, if you are religious, "God is my strength."
- Sing a happy song.
- Send love to someone or to a special group.
- Think about a pertinent story or fable. Make up an apt parable.
- Stimulate your Joy Center.

You have no excuse for dwelling on a negative thought.

OVERLAYING

Overlaying is used to replace a dislike, fear, or bad habit with a positive one. It works like this. Go into the alpha state. Picture in your mind the thing you dislike, say, being stuck in a traffic jam. Now shrink that picture to the size of a postage stamp. Then picture a pleasant scene or experience. Attach strong emotion to your pleasant scene. Hold the positive though for a few seconds and then repeat the sequence three times. Next time you get stuck in traffic, your neurological system will not react negatively because it will associate the event with the positive feelings.

Another variation is to write the thing that bothers you on a piece of paper. Close your eyes, go into alpha, and then visualize something very positive and happy. Then open your eyes and look at what you wrote on the paper. Repeat three times. Now when the negative thing comes up, it will be associated with positive emotions so that it will not bug you and you can face it objectively.

This method is useful to curb an unrealistic attraction to something like, say, chocolate candy. Close your eyes, go into the alpha state and visualize lots of chocolate candy. Reduce the size of the picture. Now visualize something of the same color as chocolate but that is disgusting. Smell the foul odor. Feel the icky, gooey, unpleasant texture. Taste it if you have the nerve. Just the thought makes you sick. You feel like you want to throw up. Repeat three times.

Anthony Robins, the positive-thinking guru, describes the use of overlaying a bit differently. He suggests you mentally picture a scene of the thing you want to change. Say you want to change a habit of overeating. You would picture yourself eating gluttonously, really making a pig of yourself. See how disgusting you look wolfing down big bites of food. Feel the sickening sensation that comes after you overeat.

Then, in the lower right corner of your mental screen, place a very small screen. In that small screen visualize yourself eating properly and quitting before you feel full. Feel good about yourself for eating this way. Feel and think about being healthy. See yourself eating properly. See yourself stopping before you feel full. Feel good about yourself for being in control. Then, quickly magnify the positive small screen and let it replace the large picture of your gluttonous eating. As you do this, say aloud, "whooooosh." Repeat the process three times. Robins claims the "whooooosh" is important.

You may have to do this a few days to reinforce the positive habit. Be sure to add strong positive emotions to the good picture.

ACTING

Acting is a powerful tool in using your subconscious mind. I already mentioned the documentary on PBS TV in which a professor claimed hypnotism was acting.

Acting as if has a huge asset. When you are acting, *everything* is logical. I could ask you to *believe* that your hand is stuck to your forearm. That is illogical and unbelievable. It would be impossible to have faith in that. But if I ask you to *act as if* your hand was stuck to your forearm, you could do that easily. Acting does not require *belief* or *faith*.

Recall that your subconscious mind finds ways to achieve the goals you give it. So if you are feeling blue, you are giving your subconscious mind the goal of being blue. Being blue is not healthy and you should not want to stay that way. But to tell your subconscious mind that you are happy may be unbelievable to you. If it is unbelievable, then you will have some fear of failure. This fear of failure will probably overpower your *will* to be happy (The Law of Reversed Effort).

But you can *act as if* you are happy. Acting as if you are happy will accomplish two goals. One, it will give your subconscious mind the goal of being happy. Two, it will send neurotransmitters from your body cells to your brain cells telling your brain that you *are* happy. Then your brain will become happy and, in turn, send neurotransmitters that will make your body feel happy. The folklore, "Act happy and you will become happy" is true. Studies prove that neurotransmitters travel both ways. When you feel happy, your subconscious mind sends messages to your body to act happy. Conversely, when your body acts happy, your body cells send messages to your brain that you *are* happy.

It is easier to *act* well when you are sick than it is to *believe* you are well. If you do not give your subconscious mind the thought, the goal of being well, it, conversely, has the goal of being sick. So learn to ACT AS IF...

ACTING ROUTINE—EXERCISE

ACTING—CONSCIOUS MIND/SUBCONSCIOUS MIND WORKING TOGETHER

Close your eyes.

Go to alpha...3...2...1..."ALPHA"

Look up about 20 degrees and see a small black dot.

Visualize the dot coming closer and getting larger and larger until it surrounds you. Surrounded by blackness, think of being in a black room.

This is your sanctuary...a place where you think with harmonic energy...energy with a singular goal...This is where you can replace bad habits and eliminate negative emotions.

Now imagine a stage in an auditorium.

You are the director and you are watching from where the audience sits.

On stage, you see yourself. You are an actor.

Then you realize there are two of you acting.

One is guided by your conscious mind; the other is guided by your subconscious mind.

They are not getting along.

They are not listening to each other.

They are fighting...they are not working together at all.

Your conscious mind is giving commands and your subconscious mind is ignoring them.

Your subconscious mind knows it can do so many things, but your conscious mind is being critical and carping.

Your conscious mind knows what is best for your body, but your subconscious mind is acting only on emotion.

You see your subconscious mind eating too much food only because it tastes good.

You see your body acting sick needlessly because of negative and false emotions.

You have seen enough as director, and you firmly yell, "Stop, enough!" You demand the following:

This is enough...no more of this bad acting!

From now on you two, conscious mind and subconscious mind, must work and act together...as a team.

From now on you must communicate constructively and lovingly.

From now on you two love each other...it is only natural...you are of the same body.

From now on you both must work lovingly for your highest good...your body's highest good...and for everybody else's good also.

From now on conscious mind is in charge...but conscious mind is a loving boss...selfless...only entertaining the thought of the highest good of subconscious mind and your precious body.

From now on, conscious mind must only entertain healthful, positive thoughts during all waking hours.

Conscious mind constantly talks to subconscious mind and guides it, and gives it positive, well thought out goals.

Subconscious mind gladly fulfills each goal in the fastest, easiest possible way.

Subconscious mind keeps your body healthy and vital...All old negative emotions are now dissolved and discarded.

Both conscious mind and subconscious mind now merge back into one body.

Now walk up to your body and enter it.

Look out through your eyes and see the stage around you.

Feel the fellowship of a conscious mind and subconscious mind that work together...and love each other.

Sense how better the world is because of this change.

See yourself—your conscious mind and subconscious mind acting together for your highest good.

Act like you can cure any ill or situation that comes up.

Act as if miracles are common in your life.

Act as though your conscious mind can accomplish anything with the aid of your subconscious mind...act as if nothing is too difficult to accomplish...act as if you have absolute faith...pure and resolute. Act like this is normal.

Now visualize a pure white, loving cloud over your head representing love, which is harmonic energy from the one source.

This cloud shifts down on you and covers you and everything around you.

You are one with yourself...you feel complete.

Now everything takes on a golden glow.

This golden glow represents harmony...harmony between your conscious mind and subconscious mind...harmony between you and the outside world...between you and your inner self.

Feel this glow and act as though you know for absolute certainty that this harmony is with you from now on.

Now go back to the black room.

See the black dissolving and becoming a black spot above your head.

See the black spot fade and disappear in the distance.

1...2...feeling refreshed and elated...3, you are wide awake. Open your eyes and smile.

Act happy and vibrant and energetic.

METHODS of Using Your Subconscious Mind, Part 3

Lesson Eight

METHODS OF USING YOUR SUBCONSCIOUS MIND, PART 3

THE CLASSIC METHOD

Before I describe the "Classic Method" of conditioning, two more tools of the subconscious mind need to be explained: "triggers" and "instant playback."

TRIGGERS AND CONDITIONED RESPONSES

Ivan Petrovich Pavlov won the Nobel Prize for his famous experiment on conditioned reflexes. Even though most readers are familiar with this experiment, it is so important that I will review it.

Pavlov showed food to a hungry dog. The dog salivated. After showing the food to the hungry dog a few times, he rang a bell at the same time he showed the food. After ringing the bell several more times while showing the food to the dog, the dog became "conditioned" to the bell. After the dog was conditioned to the bell, any time Pavlov rang the bell, the dog salivated even without the food.

In other words, the response of salivating at the sight of food was transferred to the sound of a bell, something that had nothing to do with food or hunger. There is no natural connection between a ringing bell and salivating.

Suppose a child witnesses this active, emotional scene. Her mother sees a mouse in the kitchen. She screams, gets hysterical, and runs around the kitchen chasing the mouse with a broom, knocking over a chair. For a child this is a vivid picture and full of emotion. Thirty years later when she sees a mouse her conditioned reflex is triggered and she screams and gets excited.

"Triggers" are like icons on your computer screen. They are shortcuts to lengthy programs. An example of using a trigger is this. A key to using your subconscious mind is to go into the alpha state of mind. Alpha is achieved by going through a lengthy relaxation program, like the ones presented after the previous lessons. While you were relaxed and in alpha, you were conditioned to a trigger, in one case, the word "ALPHA." After going through these exercises a few times you should become conditioned to this word. After you are conditioned, you do not have to use the full routine to go into alpha. You simply use your trigger. Take a deep breath, let it out, and visualize and say to yourself the word "ALPHA," and you bypass the relaxations routine. You are in alpha.

How many times does it take to condition yourself? Everybody is different. Some people condition themselves after only a few times, while others take longer. Moreover, the conditioning should be reinforced periodically. Again there are no hard rules. Go by your feelings or, if you must, ask your subconscious mind if the conditioning is sufficient (see Lesson Five).

Another trigger that was included in the conditioning exercises was touching the thumb and forefinger together to relax. There is no reason to be tense, even for a little while.

Even an elite athlete does not tense his entire body. He uses only the muscles necessary to do the job. Any additional tension is counterproductive. Your thumb and forefinger naturally touch many times a day. Each time they touch, your body is reminded to stay relaxed.

Norman Cousins wrote a book describing how he healed himself of a fatal disease by using laughter to stimulate his immune system. He checked out of the hospital and checked into a motel where he watched funny videos. Laughter stimulated his immune system and, obviously, kept him from getting depressed. Depression interferes with the immune system.

Cousins did not use a trigger, but it would have been a good idea. Suppose that every time he watched a funny video he looked at a symbol of a happy face. After he was conditioned to a happy face, he would only have to imagine, or see, a happy face to stimulate his immune system. He would have eliminated having to watch an entire video. He then could have hung pictures of happy faces in his home, car, and office. Every time a happy face came into view, his immune system would be stimulated.

An experiment similar to this was conducted on mice. One group of mice was injected with a chemical that stimulated the immune system and they were conditioned to the smell of camphor. Another group was injected with a chemical that retarded the immune system and they were also conditioned with the smell of camphor. So both groups were conditioned to the same trigger but with opposite responses, one to enhance and the other to retard the immune system.

Then the mice in both groups were injected with chemicals that cause cancer. When they were injected with the cancer-causing chemical, they were also exposed to the smell of camphor. The mice conditioned to stimulate the immune system by the smell resisted cancer. The mice conditioned by the same smell to retard the immune system got cancer.

A trigger, for example, for self-confidence, might be a picture of Teddy Roosevelt. Another, one I use, is a picture of a bristle cone pine tree. My health program, which takes over 15 minutes to read out loud, is conditioned to a picture of a bristle cone pine tree. Bristle cone pines have a special meaning to me. They live long and they survive under extreme conditions (high altitude, cold, heat, and drought.) To me, they are the epitome of hale and hearty. Triggers are better if they have an emotional meaning to you.

Triggers can be words, images, colors, and actions, such as touching fingers together or blinking. Sounds and odors can also be used. I also use the color green as a trigger to my health program. Each time I see, or think of, the color green, my entire health program is stimulated. I see the color green hundreds of times each day.

INSTANT PLAYBACK

Einstein is reputed to have said, "Time is relative. A minute seems like 10 seconds when a pretty girl is sitting on your lap; ten seconds seems like a minute when you are sitting on a hot stove." Time is what we perceive it to be.

The first time you drive a new route it seems unduly long. That is because everything is new. You are exposed to thousands of unfamiliar stimuli. The second time you drive the same route, it seems shorter. The same stimuli evoke fewer new impressions to fill in the time.

Relative time can be even more dramatic in the subconscious mind. This is illustrated in an experiment conducted at a Midwestern university. A group of students was hypnotized and asked to pick the fruit off a given number of trees. I do not have the details of the experiment but assume it was a peach orchard of 100 trees and each tree had 10 peaches.

The first time they picked the peaches it took them, say, 10 minutes. The experiment was repeated with the same students. The second time, they picked the fruit in a minute. The experiment was repeated a third time. This time the students picked the same amount of fruit in one second.

Lecron reported a similar experiment. He hypnotized a lady and asked her to review the movie *Gone With the Wind* in her mind, an emotional movie she had seen several times. When she finished reviewing the movie, she was to drop her hand as a signal she was done. She dropped her hand almost immediately. Lecron woke her and told her he meant for her to review the *entire* movie. She said she did!

Once a neurological pattern is ingrained in our brain, such as recalling picking an orchard of fruit or an emotional movie we have seen several times, our subconscious minds can review the entire ingrained pattern in a flash. This is "instant playback."

You will use this time compression feature, instant playback, to your advantage later in this lesson.

BACKGROUND

I believe classic conditioning is the best method for conditioning crucial programs in your subconscious mind, such as health, success, and personality traits. Classic conditioning is easy but it takes a little more time than the other methods because an affirmation has to be prepared. First, a couple of

points need to be reviewed. You do not *change* programs in your subconscious mind; you *replace* them. Your subconscious mind can accept only one of two or more concepts as true. If your subconscious mind has been conditioned to believe you are shy, then you need to condition your subconscious mind with a new program—one that will give you poise and self-confidence. If your subconscious mind has been programmed to believe you will get one or more colds every winter, get a headache under every stressful condition, and are prone to get sick, then you need to program your subconscious mind to hold the concept of being healthy, hearty, hale, and having an immune system that is strong and keeps you well.

If someone is 50 years old, his or her subconscious mind probably has 50 years of conditioning the concept it now holds true. To overcome those 50 years of conditioning in a short time, a very efficient way is needed. The conditioning must be done in the alpha state, it must be done using a comprehensive affirmation, and it must be repeated until it is the dominant thought in your subconscious mind.

It will take more than once to condition your subconscious mind with a new concept for it to become stronger than the existing negative one. Everybody is different, so there are no finite rules for how many times you have to condition your subconscious mind with the new program. My suggestion is once or twice a day for a week, then once a week for a month, then once a month for a year, and then once or twice a year.

STEP ONE—WRITE AN AFFIRMATION

The affirmation should be broad to cover every aspect of the new concept you want in your subconscious mind. I wrote a general affirmation for "health" for an example, which is given at the end of this lesson. The affirmation itself is over seven pages long. Staying healthy is important so you want

to be certain that you replace every negative concept in your subconscious mind with a positive, healthy one.

Use the affirmation in this lesson as a starting point. Tailor it to your needs; shorten it or add to it. Use images that mean something to you. For example, when affirming the filtering capability of your kidneys, you might use one of the following images. If you are a chemist, you might picture an elaborate chemistry laboratory with complex filtering technology. If you are a homemaker, you might picture pouring orange juice through a sieve or fine cloth to remove the seeds and pulp.

WORDING

Words, for the most part, are the tools of the conscious mind. Words are your tool to create an affirmation for the subconscious mind. So keep in mind that these words are used to evoke *images* and *feelings.* Use words to describe action and to paint vivid scenes that evoke strong emotions.

"I am healthy" is nice but something like the following is better:

"I see myself with a radiant glow walking briskly in a beautiful park planted with bright-colored flowers. I see yellow pansies with delicate stems and sturdy blue daffodils as I walk by. My step is fast and I feel as though I am floating. I relish life. I enjoy life fully. I enjoy the beauty of nature. I feel one with nature. I feel a vital life force coursing through my body as tiny dancing bolts of lightning. I am happy. I see myself with a wide grin as I walk, knowing that I am alive and well and hearty and vigorous. My happiness and good nature stimulate my immune system. I visualize my cells talking with each other and with my subconscious mind with tiny cell phones. I thank my cells for communicating with my immune system and for staying healthy and for functioning for the good of my body.

"I picture my white cells patrolling my body for unwelcome foreign bacteria, viruses, and anything that is not there for my best health. When they spot an unwelcome microbe, they attack and annihilate it like little Pac Men, gobbling all the bad guys in sight. I see macrophages as super tiny vacuum cleaners coming in and cleaning up. I see them keeping my blood pure and healthy. My immune system has a humongous hard drive that recognizes millions of foreign substances and my immune cells get rid of them as soon as they enter my bloodstream. My immune system is magnificent. I love it. I thank it." (You could animate your immune system by giving it shape and a voice. Then you could talk to it directly.)

"I feel my heart pumping blood throughout my body easily, effortlessly. I sense that my heart is strong and powerful. I see the corpuscles delivering nourishment to every cell. It gladly pumps blood and nourishment to every cell of my body. I now thank my heart for serving me faithfully. I visualize my heart with a smile. It is happy and loves to pump nourishment to all my cells. My arteries and blood vessels are wide open and flexible. The blood that they carry supplies each and every cell and organ with all the nourishment they need to function at peak level. My blood carries away all waste to maintain healthy cells. I bless my heart and the blood that it pumps,...," etc., etc.

Thank and bless all of the cells, organs, bones, and everything else in your body. Embellish! Exaggerate. Emote. Lay it on. Get carried away. Forget what you learned in writing class. Your affirmation does not have to be logical. You do not even have to use good grammar. It should cover as much as you can think of and it must make you *see* and *feel* what you are talking about.

BE REALISTIC

Be bold in what you want to accomplish but being unrealistic may cause discouragement and loss of confidence. If you like to play tennis, are a "B" player, and 72 years old, having a goal of winning a Wimbledon championship would be unrealistic. Seek excellence, not perfection.

An exception to being "realistic" is healing an ailment. I believe anything is possible concerning health. Spontaneous healings have been documented. These spontaneous healings were due to a mental process, not a medical one. One study, conducted by Elmer and Alyce Green, showed that the commonality of spontaneous healings in the study was a *change in attitude*. By all means use these methods but never use them in place of professional help. Use them in concert with professional help.

USE THE PRESENT TENSE

The subconscious mind functions only in the present. When you say, "I will get better." You will get better tomorrow but tomorrow never gets here. Tomorrow is always one day away.

"I will get better" tacitly states that you are not now well. So this statement gives your subconscious mind a goal of not being well now.

Give your subconscious mind the goal of *being* well. Say and picture yourself as being well *now*—no matter what your present condition is.

BE POSITIVE

Many successful gurus sometimes use negative affirmations. I would argue, however, that negative affirmations should never be used, and I will give you several reasons why.

Visualizing a negative is often difficult. Picture, for example, "Michael Jordan did not play basketball today." Seeing someone not doing something is difficult.

Some psychologists believe that the subconscious mind does not see the "not." Thus, when you say, "I am not afraid," your subconscious mind hears "I am afraid."

On the other hand, another school believes that any adjective in front of a noun emphasizes it in the subconscious mind. If they are correct, then the "not" in "I am not afraid" emphasizes "afraid" in your subconscious mind.

Once you say and visualize a word in association with something, it is difficult to forget that word. Close your eyes, relax and picture this: The door to the room you are in opens and a pink elephant enters. The elephant has on a silly party hat and is blowing a horn. The elephant prances around the room and steps on your foot. It hurts! Now forget the elephant. You cannot. If you vividly imagined that scene, you cannot forget that zany, pink, party-loving elephant.

A greedy king offered a fortune to anyone who could show him how to turn sand to gold. A clever sorcerer used a trick to make it appear that he turned sand into gold. He gave the king a sham method for turning sand into gold. Then the sorcerer told the king that he must never, never think of the word "abracadabra" while turning sand into gold. Of course, the king could not get that word off his mind every time he tried to turn sand to gold. Thus, he could not blame the sorcerer for his failure.

So do not use a negative such as, "I am not afraid" because you emphasize being afraid and place "being afraid" in your mind. It is just as easy to say, "I am poised and confident." The above reasons should convince you to use positive affirmations, not negative ones.

BE SPECIFIC AND LITERAL

When making up a picture of something you want, be specific. The vision you evoke by saying, "I see myself getting a new car" is weak compared with saying, "I see my new car. It is a blue Volvo S70 4-door sedan. I can feel the pressure on my toe as I kick the tires. I see myself sitting at the wheel. The upholstery is beige leather. I smell the new leather. I turn on the CD/cassette/radio and listen to the stereophonic music of the Beatles coming from the six speakers. I see myself driving along Route 66. I marvel how smooth my car rides. I see the scenery through the car window. I just passed a red barn..." etc.

PERSONALIZE IT

An affirmation in your words is better than one written by someone else. The words and images you paint will have more connotations and meanings to you. It will have more power. Plagiarize affirmations, but edit and personalize them. Doctor them up with *your* feelings and attitudes.

STRESS ACTIVITY

See yourself *doing* and *being*. "I am poised under all conditions. I see myself acting courageously in an emergency. I am alert and go into action. I see myself calmly calling the Fire Department. I recall where the fire extinguisher is and I go into action putting out the fire. I instruct everybody else to get out of the house. I see that those around me admire my calm, bold actions. I feel confident..." etc.

USE ALL OF YOUR SENSES

Use words that make you *hear, smell, taste,* and *feel.* "I see the look of understanding on my boss's face as I ask him for a raise. His eyes twinkle and he smiles at me and tells me

I am doing a superb job. I feel elation when he gives me a raise and a bonus. I hear him congratulate me and say how much I deserve it. I can taste the champagne and feel the bubbles tickling my nose as my wife and I drink to my success."

BE EMOTIONAL

Emotion is energy. Get excited. "I am so happy that tears are running down my cheek...I gladly...I enjoy...I excitedly...I feel strongly...I am sooo happy," etc.

PERMISSIVE VS. AUTHORITATIVE

A permissive affirmation is, "You may relax," or "I now allow my arms to relax." An authoritative affirmation is "Relax!" or "I command my arms to relax now!" Both are effective. I suggest that the permissive type of wording is better if it get results. If your subconscious mind does not comply, then use the authoritative affirmation. Your subconscious mind must obey, but you want to establish a mutual, loving relationship. Friends or lovers do not command each other; they do not have to. They work together out of mutual respect and need.

I knew someone who was not getting cooperation from his subconscious mind. He went into the alpha state and berated his subconscious mind for not cooperating. He said that it was imperative that they work together for both their sakes. They lived in the same body and it was to their interest to keep that body healthy. Being emotionally healthy depends on single-mindedness. Internal turmoil is unhealthy, causes stress, and is counterproductive. He went on for minutes; it was a real heart-to-heart scolding. He claimed he was "out of sorts" for a few days but after that, his conscious mind and subconscious mind got along fine.

STEP TWO—ATTACH A TRIGGER

Attach a "trigger" to your affirmation. Every time you condition your subconscious mind, attach a trigger to it. I used the color green as one of my triggers for health. Near the end of the affirmation I say, "Each and every time I see or picture the color "GREEN," this affirmation is repeated a thousand times. Each time I see or picture in my mind the color "GREEN," this affirmation is reinforced and affirmed and acted on. Each time I see or think of the color "GREEN," this affirmation is magnified, enhanced, and energized over and over."

I chose the color green because I associate it with life, new growth, and health. I hung a sheet of green paper in my closet. After awhile my conscious mind ignores it but my subconscious mind sees it many times a day. Fortunately the color green is abundant, so my affirmation is energized hundreds of times every day.

STEP THREE—PLANT YOUR AFFIRMATION

You can imbed your affirmation in your subconscious mind in two ways. One, go into the alpha state and read it aloud. See it, speak it, and hear it. Command your subconscious mind to accept your affirmation and confirm it as you go into a deeper state of alpha. Then go deeper and preferably deep enough where you lose consciousness. When you are unconscious, your picky conscious mind cannot interfere.

The other method is to record your affirmation on tape. If you have not conditioned yourself to go into deep alpha in a short time, include a relaxation routine at the beginning. Turn on your tape player and go into a deep alpha. Go into the state using the word "RELAX." This routine (at the end of Lesson Four) uses the word "sleep" in it. You will not go to

sleep; you will go into deep alpha and be unconscious. There is no word in English that means, "Go into the alpha or theta state and lose consciousness" so we are stuck with using the word "sleep." Your subconscious mind knows what you want because of your *expectation* and *faith* that you will go into deep alpha. Going into a sleep state is best because your conscious mind is not able to interfere with the suggestions.

STEP FOUR—REPEAT

As a rule of thumb, repeat the affirmation every day for a week, every week for a month, every month for a year, and then, every year.

STEP FIVE—GROUPING AFFIRMATIONS

A lot of time can be saved by grouping affirmations and by using the "instant playback" technique. A suggested grouping might be to use a different fruit, flower, or color as a trigger for each affirmation. For example, you could use:

- An apple for your "Health" affirmation

- A pear for "Success"

- A bunch of grapes for "Relationships"

- A banana for "Abundance"

- A papaya for "Nutrition" and proper eating habits

After you condition yourself to these triggers, they can all be activated in your subconscious mind in seconds. Go into alpha and picture yourself placing each fruit sequentially in a basket or better, coming out of a cornucopia. Any time you are in alpha just take a few seconds to picture each fruit and you have repeated the five affirmations in total in only seconds.

HEALTH AFFIRMATION CONDITIONING EXERCISE

This is an example of a generic affirmation. It is intended to bring your subconscious mind to the foreground and saturate it with concepts of excellent health. Use this affirmation as a starting point. Doctor it up so it expresses *your* emotions and feelings about health. Change it, add to it, cut some sections out—make it represent you. You can think of more parts and functions of your body that you want to fortify and bless. And remember, use phrases that conjure something you can visualize. Robust health should be thought of as natural and continuous.

A relaxation routine is placed at the start to take you into a deep state of alpha. When you can go into alpha in a few seconds using your trigger word, you can remove that section from the affirmation. Now, record it, sit in a comfortable chair, close your eyes, and playback the tape. Or, get comfortable in an easy chair, go into alpha, read it aloud, tell yourself that this affirmation is embedded in your subconscious mind at every level and at every age as you take yourself into a deeper state of mind. Then use the "RELAX" trigger to go into an unconscious alpha state.

HEALTH AFFIRMATION

I am about to experience deep relaxation. Because relaxation makes me feel good, I eagerly look forward to this routine and going into deep alpha and theta states. I like and desire the feeling of contentment it gives me. I can see myself in a state of bliss and enjoying it. Relaxation is so good for me. It restores and energizes me. It frees me of tension and allows perfect circulation in every part of my body. My body anticipates that feeling and desires to relax, relax deeply, ever so deeply and naturally. My eyelids close naturally and as they close, I feel a wave of warmth sweep over me from my head to toes.

I now become aware of my breathing. I notice that it is slowing and deepening. I imagine that I can actually see the molecules of air that I breathe in. I see and know that each molecule is energy...the energy of life...each molecule contains the energy of the life force. I see this energy as tiny sparklers. I see a field of tiny sparks. These microscopic sparks enter my lungs and energize me...rejuvenate me...fill me with positive energy and vitality. This energy sizzles within me. I see this energy entering my lungs and being carried to every cell in my body. My body welcomes it and uses it with gusto. I thank the life force for energizing and rejuvenating my body.

When I exhale, I see the molecules of air carry out waste...negative energy...everything that I no longer need. When I exhale, I see a cloud of gray exiting my body. These molecules of air also carry out with them tension and all anxiety, and I feel myself relaxing...growing more and more content with my body and my life.

I now visualize myself walking on the shore of a tropical island. The water is calm. The temperature is perfect and there is a gentle breeze coming off the ocean. Someone has carved a seat with a backrest in the sand. I gently sit in the seat and feel the soft, warm sand cradle my body. It feels so good to just sit here and let go...I let go of thoughts of my life for a few minutes...let go and simply live in this minute...let go and simply be aware of now and the beauty around me. All cares and thoughts of tomorrow and yesterday vanish from my mind. I am here and this instant

is the only time on my mind. I allow my eyes to gaze at the cumulus clouds above me. I realize how giant they are. They constantly change shape. I am having fun imaging what the shapes remind me of.

In order to enjoy this moment more, and to go into a deeper, healthy, natural state of mind, I now relax even more. I am now twice as relaxed as a minute ago. As I observe the clouds, I feel my body getting heavier and heavier. This is the feeling of complete relaxation. I relish the scene in front of me...the white billowy clouds, the gentle surf, the distant horizon, and the relaxing blue-green colors of the ocean. I notice my breathing is slow and in tune with the surf washing up on the shore.

I now become aware of my feet and legs and let them relax twice again as much. I now move my focus on my buttocks, hips, and torso. I ask them each in a kind way to relax more. As I do so I feel the weight of my body increase as my muscles let go of all tension, unwind and become limp...ever so limp. I now ask my arms and hands to relax. I feel my shoulders slump from the added weight of my arms. Lastly, I ask my head and shoulders to completely relax. They comply. My throat and neck muscles are relaxed and devoid of tension. My tongue relaxes and the voice inside me quiets. I feel sooo good.

I am now eager for this affirmation. It is not necessary for my conscious mind to hear it. This affirmation, these concepts about health, sink into my subconscious mind—every part of it—naturally and deeply. The neurological pathways that are created are my only truths. I feel strongly about this. I can feel this emotion power the pathways of this affirmation in my brain. My subconscious mind eagerly accepts this affirmation as the only truth and this truth overpowers all other thoughts, concepts, and feelings about health. My subconscious mind accepts it because it is for our best health and general good. As I hear the count from 10 to 1, I slip down, deeper and deeper into a natural healthy level of theta. 10...9...8...down and down...deeper and deeper...6...5...4...3. I am in deep theta, going even deeper now. 2...1. I am at my deepest level. I now accept the following affirmation with delight.

My conscious mind has faded and my subconscious mind surfaces ready and eager to accept these affirmations. I see myself with a radiant glow walking briskly in a beautiful garden planted with bright colored flowers. I see yellow pansies with delicate stems and sturdy blue daffodils as I walk by. I feel exhilarated. I feel tingling throughout my body from the life force within me. I feel the life force of good and health flow though my body and mind. I feel at one with nature. I feel and see my life force in my body as a glow of vibrant, tingling energy. My step is fast and I feel as though I am floating. I relish life. I enjoy life fully. I am happy. I see myself with a wide grim. I walk knowing that I am alive and well and vital and energetic. I am walking vigorously. I see myself enjoying being active. Being active makes me feel good and it is good for me. Activity keeps me healthy and young. I am the ever-renewing, ever-unfolding, expression of life.

My subconscious mind is now completely receptive to all body-, mind-, and health-building suggestions. My subconscious mind accepts only suggestions that are positive and for my best good. These suggestions work within me day and night, 24 hours a day to make me stronger physically and emotionally...healthier and happier. They work within me while my body is awake or asleep, at all times. I now make the following suggestions mine. My subconscious mind eagerly accepts them for my conscious mind's and subconscious mind's best health and well being.

I think only positive thoughts. I forgive myself for anything I have done to my body in the past. I think of my body only as I now want it to be. I think of my body only as it is in my mind—whole, pure, hearty, hale, active, lively, brimming with energy, and at a healthy weight. I resolve to eat healthy foods and eat only enough to maintain my highest health and energy. I see myself eating healthful foods and in small quantities. I avoid sugar and white flour. I enjoy a sweet now and then but only in small amounts. I see myself refusing a second piece of candy. I easily control the amount of sweets I eat. I refuse to keep eating just because the food tastes good. I control the quantity of food I eat. I eat a well-rounded, balanced diet. I picture myself eating lots of vegetables and fruits and leaving the table after I have eaten enough. I stop eating long before I feel full. I know that it

takes about ten minutes to feel full so I stop long before I feel full at the table. My body shies from fatty foods. I feel good about myself because I now eat to maintain my highest health. It gives me a feeling of self-control. I see myself with abundant energy. I see this energy vibrating and sizzling throughout my body.

It is unimportant what I thought in the past. I release wrong concepts about eating and health and release their effects on me. I now feel and see myself as healthy and radiant. I feel the life energy pulse throughout my body now. Every cell, every gland, every muscle, every organ, is now flushed with life and vitality. From now on I constantly see myself as healthy and happy. I think only positively about myself.

There is intelligence in me that created me from two tiny cells. This intelligence knows how to form bones and flesh and organs and the brain I think with. This intelligence still lives and functions in every cell of my body. This intelligence has a strong will for me to be healthy and live a useful and happy life. This intelligence is behind every activity in my body. It loves what it does and is happy to serve me. It functions every second, every day of my life. This intelligence provides me with everything I need to stay healthy. It provides my body with an immune system that keeps me healthy and fights off all foreign microbes that enter my body. It knows how to stop bleeding in cuts and it knows how to heal and grow new skin. This intelligence that permeates my body can manufacture any substance my body needs to be healthy and vibrant. It knows how to control all the functions going on in my body. This intelligence initiates and monitors the billions of functions that occur every second of my life throughout my body. I call on this inner intelligence to keep me healthy and vigorous. I allow this inner knowing to work for my physical and mental well being. I thank this internal intelligence for serving me so well. I thank it over and over again and send it love.

I am relaxed and calm. My body is at rest. Relaxation allows my blood to flow freely throughout my body. I see and feel my blood coursing through my body bringing fresh nutrients to all my cells. I visualize it carrying everything my cells need to stay healthy. In my mind I see my blood carrying minuscule fruits

and vegetables and other healthy foods to every cell. I also see my blood carrying away waste. It keeps my cells healthy and my body clean. Older, tired cells gladly transcend life and leave my body so that only fresh, healthy cells remain. I am strong and well and vigorous now. I feel good. I see myself dancing joyfully. I feel love in every cell. I actually visualize tiny hearts of vibrating red representing love flowing through my veins blessing every cell. My blood flows easily through even my tiniest vein. I thank my blood for keeping my cells healthy in every part of my body. I thank it for making thousands of new blood cells every minute to maintain this flow of nutrients in and waste products out. I visualize happy faces on every cell in my body. My cells are happy and loved. I only send them positive energy in the form of thoughts.

My immune system is magnificent. It remembers thousands and thousands of unwelcome microbes. When it encounters one, it sends messages to my subconscious mind and my subconscious mind sends an army of white cells, killer T-cells, B-cells, and all the rest of its arsenal. These cells destroy all unhealthy cells and microbes. My immune system then sends in macrophages to clean up. It is a miraculous system and it works automatically and naturally and it works for me 24 hours each day. I visualize this as a war zone—a war on all things that do not belong in my body. I visualize this action as a video game. The good guys blast away and rid the world of the bad guys. I see tiny Pac Men coursing through my veins and arteries eating up all those unwelcome cells, unhealthy cells, and microbes. I thank my immune system for the magnificent job it does 24 hours a day, year after year.

My happiness enhances and causes my immune system to perform even better. I know medical research has proven that good nature and joyfulness enhances my immune system. I therefore maintain a happy mood and keep up a good nature. Every time I am at my happiest mood I visualize a Happy Face symbol. I associate a Happy Face symbol with happiness. So every time I see or think about a Happy Face my immune system is invigorated, enhanced, and energized. Every time I see or visualize a Happy Face, my

immune system is renewed and energized. Happy Faces keep me healthy and well.

I now visualize my heart. It is a strong and durable and tough muscle. It pumps continuously and vigorously all day, day after day. I thank my heart for sending blood to every cell in my body. I thank it for beating rhythmically and forcibly. I can see it as a metronome that always keeps perfect rhythm. My heart loves to pump blood and it does it joyously. I picture my heart as playful and enjoying the work it does. I can actually see a smile on the middle of it. It pumps effortlessly and happily. It pumps blood that purifies and energizes my body all day and all night. I thank it for serving me so well.

All the arteries that supply my heart with blood are relaxed and clear. The intelligence in me does not allow cells to condense and coalesce on the walls of these arteries. These arteries are wide open. I see them as plastic tubing. I can see the blood flow through them effortlessly, carrying life-sustaining oxygen and nutrients to my heart, which in turn thanks the arteries.

I now focus on my lungs. I actually see and hear and feel large volumes of air coming in and going out. I see the incoming air as white, vibrating, tingling energy. This energy is picked up by my blood and carried throughout my body. My lungs bring in this vital energy constantly and happily. I can see it and feel it. This energy tingles and invigorates me. I feel my entire body tingling with energy. I feel more rested and vital with every breath. Slow, even, deep, breathing relaxes me and comforts me. I feel a comforting well-being. I feel peace in my body. I thank my lungs for providing me with life and energy.

My bronchi are wide open and ignore all pollutants that flow in and out with the air. These microscopic foreign invaders are simply ignored and allowed to past in and out. They are inert and my immune system ignores them because they part of my environment and are harmless to me now.

I now proceed to give strength and harmony to my digestive system. My stomach is strong, resilient and it rebuilds itself constantly. My stomach digests my food with ease. I maintain a

happy attitude while I eat because it allows my stomach to work more efficiently. I assist my stomach by keeping a cheerful, buoyant spirit. I transfer this joyful, buoyant attitude to my stomach while I eat and after I eat while it is digesting the food. I visualize a sophisticated laboratory with beakers, and distillation bottles, and flasks, and all the other things used in an advanced biological laboratory. My digestive system manufactures the chemicals needed to digest my food and allow it to transverse to my blood where it travels to every cell in my body. All my cells are receiving these nutrients in the form they need. My digestive system does all of this effortlessly and with joy. I thank and bless my digestive system.

I visualize a special furnace that burns brightly and burns within me. I now visualize this furnace. I see the flames. I see reds, oranges, and yellows in the flames and in the reflections dancing off the walls and ceiling. I feel the heat. My muscles are metabolizing my nutrients. Food is used for energy. This energy is always available. I see someone tending the furnace. It is my subconscious mind. I notice that no matter how much fuel is put into the furnace it is burned up, causing the flames to dance higher and brighter. I recognize and associate the furnace as the metabolism continually going on in my body. The fuel is the food I eat, and the flames, the lovely dancing flames, signify energy. The food I eat is turned into vibrant, dynamic energy. Nothing is stored. I know my subconscious mind controls every cell, every organ every gland in my body. It controls and regulates my metabolism. I look again into the fire and notice a bed of embers. As I sleep at night these embers burn ridding my body of excess calories. Excess food is burned up. Excess calories are burned and escape as heat. My subconscious mind keeps only what is needed for my highest health and well-being. I thank my digestive system and my subconscious mind for controlling these processes effortlessly and joyfully.

My elimination system works in harmony with my digestive system. All unneeded waste products are flushed out by my blood and disposed through my intestines. My intestines keep me supplied with nutrients and allow unneeded food to pass through

easily and effortlessly. I thank my elimination system for working in harmony with my digestive system and for removing all toxins from my body. In order to assist this function I drink lots of water. I visualize myself holding up a half-gallon container. It is empty because I drank all the water. Water is good for me. I reject drinking soda and other useless carbonated drinks and drink water instead. When I think of or see a can or bottle of soda, I picture a symbol of a circle with a slash across it. From now on I prefer water. My body is composed of over 70 % water. This body water needs to be continually replaced and refreshed. My body water is like a magnet that attracts fresh water. Consequently, I constantly feel an urge to drink water.

I visualize my kidneys as the most perfect filters every made. They happily filter impurities from the fluids that nourish my entire body. I visualize dirty water passing though my kidneys and coming out pure and transparent. My kidneys keep my body fluids clean and pure. I thank them and send love to them in the form of a white, vibrating cloud of tingling energy. The cloud surrounds them and invigorates them and infuses them with vitality.

I now thank all of my joints for serving me well. I thank the intelligence in my subconscious mind that supplies them with lubricants. I visualize this now. I see myself with an oil can lubricating my knees and hips and all other joints with a super, unique lubricant. My joints are now agile and smooth working. I see a cushion between the bones and the lubricant penetrates this cushion and allows my joints to move freely and effortlessly and easily. I thank the intelligence in my subconscious mind for continuing to refurbish these cushions and keep my joints free to move effortlessly and easily.

I visualize all of my organs working together cheerfully, lovingly. We realize that we are all working together for our body, our good, our well-being. I thank my subconscious mind for controlling and regulating the millions of processes that go on in my body every moment. I see all of us working in harmony as a symphony orchestra. My subconscious mind is the conductor regulating the symphony. The music my body produces is the

most beautiful music I have ever heard. It is spellbinding; it is spiritual. All the musicians are playing together in harmony and at the correct beat. My body is a symphony orchestra. Synchronized, every part working in unison, producing melodic music. I hear my body's song.

I accept and imprint this affirmation deeply in all levels and all locations in my mind. It is strong and overpowers all other thoughts and concepts about health. My subconscious mind accepts these concepts at every age level. I now imagine that I am one year old. I see myself cradled in my mother's arms. I look at myself at this age and realize how helpless I am and how dependent I am on others. No matter what ideas and concepts I might have learned I now realize there is some innate knowledge within me that tells me I am a healthy baby and I will always be healthy. Even though I cannot understand the words of this affirmation, somehow, I sense the meaning and it dominates my mind.

I am now five years old. I can see myself in my room playing with a toy. My adult self asks this little child to believe and accept this affirmation and make it his own, and to allow it to dominate all thoughts about health. I explain this affirmation is for his good and that it is important to accept it. My entire entity at five years old smiles and agrees to do it.

I see myself as ten years old now. I see myself in the backyard playing alone. I see my adult self walk up to this young boy and ask him if I can tell him something important. He smiles and says, "Yes." I ask him to accept this affirmation and make it his and let it impress on his mind to overwhelm all false thoughts that he may have mistakenly picked up. I tell him that accepting this affirmation will allow him to play as hard and long as he wants. I tell him this affirmation will allow him to enjoy life and enable him to play hard and enjoy it. He readily agrees to accept it and believes it with his entire mind and in its entirety.

I now know that this affirmation is stronger than all negative, counterproductive, unhealthy ideas on health. It completely dominates my thoughts of health at all levels and ages of my subconscious mind.

Each and every time I think or see the color GREEN this affirmation is renewed. Each and every time I see or visualize the color GREEN this affirmation is repeated a thousand times and enhanced and energized. My subconscious mind picks up the color GREEN everywhere. Each time it sees GREEN this affirmation is emphasized and magnified. This affirmation is now part of me. It dominates my subconscious mind. It is my dominant concept of my health. It is now the dominating concept of health in my subconscious mind. My subconscious mind releases the effect of any concepts contrary to this new concept. I thank and bless these old concepts but they are now obsolete, sterile, and effete. They are useless to me now. I accept this new concept. I accept this entire affirmation for my best good health, physical and mental. My subconscious mind accepts it fully and joyfully and completely. I thank my subconscious mind for accepting it and acting on it. Excellent health, vibrant living, energetic activity is now my way of life.

Now, with a sense of gratitude, with a warm heart, with love for myself and others, I now return to the awake state on the count of "3." "1"...feeling refreshed and joyful..."2"...feeling happy and healthy..."3"...I am wide awake.

YOUR SUPERMARKET

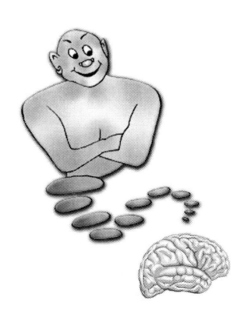

Epilogue

"YOUR SUPERMARKET"

Imagine the following:

As your instructor, I invite you to come with me to a supermarket. Standing outside you can see that the store is huge. I invite you in and I explain that the store is full of self-help materials of all kinds. There are special foods for maintaining hale and hearty health. There are books with instructions for achieving success in all phases of your life, for replacing bad habits with positive, healthful ones, for becoming at peace with those around you and with the world, for becoming more poised and self-assured, for becoming financially comfortable, and more. There are assistants to help you. This store is full of aromas to remind you to stay happy and joyful. I explain that you are entitled to everything you want. You are given a large cart. Go ahead and take all that you intend to use. Fill up your cart. If you fill your cart, an assistant will get another cart for you.

After your carts are full, you go to the checkout station where you are reminded that every thing has already been paid for.

Just as you are about to leave you have second thoughts. Maybe all of this is more trouble than it is worth. You think of the hassle to transfer it to your car and then to your home. And there will be some, though not much, effort to put it to use. So you decide to leave it there and go home without it.

You are now home and you sit in a comfortable chair and daydream. You realize that your decision to leave those resource materials was rash. The use of all those resources will help you achieve your dreams. Maybe they really do work.

You jump out of your chair and race back to the superstore. Your cart is still there. But in place of all the bulky resource materials, and in place of all the helpful assistants, there is just this book. Now you realize how easy it is to put your genie to work for your best health and welfare. You grab this book and cradle it as if it was worth all the gold in the world. This instruction book is the key to your most valuable resource, your subconscious mind— YOUR GENIE. Use the knowledge in this book and cherish your genie.

LIFE is soooooo
GOOD !

Sequel Lesson

PRAYER

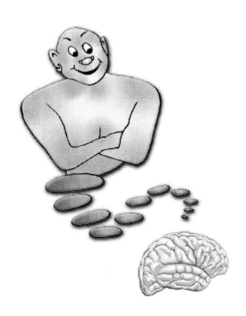

Sequel Lesson

PRAYER

"Someday…the scientists of the world will turn their laboratories over to the study of God and prayer and the spiritual forces which as yet have hardly been scratched. When this day comes, the world will see more advancement in one generation than it has seen in the past four."

—The Spindrift Group

INTRODUCTION

I believe most people would like to think prayer works but are skeptical because, it seems to them, it works so seldom. Prayer is successful, however, more than the skeptics realize. Larry Dossey, M.D. searched the scientific literature and found 124 studies on prayer. The type of prayer studied in the literature was affirmative prayer for healing or better health. Results in over half the studies showed prayer worked—based on scientific criteria. Wouldn't it be a boon if all medications were more than fifty percent effective, had no side affects, and were free!

One study has been recently reported in newspapers and magazines, as well as in one of Dr. Dossey's books. Cardiologist Randolph Byrd, a practicing Christian, conducted

the experiment. Half of 393 cardiac patients were prayed for by various religious groups for ten months. The people praying knew only the name of the patient, and neither doctors nor patients knew which patients were being prayed for. No records were kept on how the prayers were conducted. Results showed the prayed-for patients were:

- Five times less likely to require antibiotics.
- Three times less likely to develop pulmonary edema.
- None required endotracheal intubation, while twelve in the not prayed-for group did.
- Fewer died.

The subject not addressed in the scientific literature was *how* to pray. I am going to make suggestions on how to pray and make your prayers infinitely more powerful. These suggestions are based on principles carried over from the earlier lessons.

This lesson is offered with humility. No doubt there are many effective ways to pray. Success has much to do with the person's relationship with God, passion, belief, and intent. So I am not saying this is the only way to pray, but I think you can significantly increase the effectiveness of your prayers by adopting these suggestions.

In the preceding lessons, you learned how you can use your conscious mind to plant suggestions in your subconscious mind. In turn, your subconscious mind works out ways to produce results, such as a better job, a change in behavior, improved health, etc. The same logic and methodology apply in prayer except that you use a higher level of mind. A higher level is superior, and necessary, because a problem (physical, emotional, or financial) cannot be solved at the level it is created.

God cannot be described, and any description would limit God. So I am not saying this higher level of mind *is* God: just

consider this higher level of mind as some aspect of God. I will refer to this higher level of mind as Universal Mind.

UNIVERSAL MIND

Universal Mind relates to conscious mind and subconscious mind as follows. Conscious mind and subconscious mind can be described by picturing a small circle with a larger circle drawn around it. The large circle contains eleven times the area of the small circle. The small circle represents the conscious mind and the large circle represents the subconscious mind. The conscious mind and subconscious mind are located inside you. The conscious mind and subconscious mind cannot know anything that they have not seen (or imagined), been taught, or experienced. The Universal Mind, on the other hand, exists inside *and* outside of you, transcends time and space, contains all knowledge, and is common to everyone. Think of the Universal Mind as a wireless Internet, universal in scope. Think of it as the Internet of the Universe, or *Uninet* for short.

You can think of the Universal Mind as separate from God or as a part of God. It makes no difference to the law. The law works either way and it works even if you do not believe in Universal Mind. Think of an analogy of something familiar. You do not have to believe in, or even know about gravity for it to work.

Consider the following partial list of circumstantial evidence that supports this concept of a Universal Mind:

- "Remote Viewing," also called "mental telepathy," has been studied and documented.[1] In a typical experiment, a sender concentrates on a picture and

---

[1] *The Mind Race,* by Russel Targ and Keith Harary, and *Psychic Discoveries Behind the Iron Curtain,* by Shilla Ostraner and Lyn Shroeder, to name just two sources.

a receiver sits quietly with the *intent* of receiving the image from the sender. The sender and receiver can be a world apart and they can be encased in metal cages that stop electromagnetic waves. The receiver picks up on the thought and draws a reasonable rendition of the sender's picture. Some people are naturally good at telepathy but anyone can do it with practice and knowing how. The keys, in my opinion, are 1) intent, and 2) being in the alpha state.

Distance and time are not a factor in remote viewing. The inference is that we are operating in a continuous field of superior intelligence, a Uninet, a Universal Mind.

- Edgar Cayce diagnosed thousands of people while in a trance (no doubt in deep alpha or theta). If you have never heard of Edgar Cayce check out the many books about him in public libraries. There is also a host of information about him on the Internet. There are 20,000 cases of his diagnoses on record at the Edgar Cayce Library, Virginia Beach, Virginia. Most of the diagnoses were confirmed by doctors. Cases not confirmed were often due to extenuating circumstances, such as, death of the patient, inaccessibility to a doctor, or inadequate diagnostic instruments and medical knowledge. Edgar Cayce knew only the patient's location (who could be anyplace in the world) and name. Cayce could only get this information from a field of intelligence common to himself and the patient, a Universal Mind.

- Carloline Myss, a contemporary author, lecturer, and medical intuitive, claims 98 percent accuracy, which is confirmed by medical doctors. Moreover, many

ordinary people have correctly diagnosed patients. I have even done it and so have many graduates of the Basic Silva Course (Silva International, El Paso, TX.) This can be done only by tuning into a higher intelligence. The keys for tuning in to the Universal Mind are intent, being in a deep state of alpha, and practice.

- Dowsing has been practiced for centuries, if not millennia. Dowsers use a dowsing tool, which is often a forked willow branch or bent coat hangers. Dowsers typically look for water sources, water lines, and gas lines, but dowsing is not limited to these items. Dowsing cannot be performed by the subconscious mind. The subconscious mind does not know where water, water lines, gas lines, etc. are located. This knowledge has to come from intelligence outside the dowser's mind.

- The pendulum and muscle response testing have been used to get information from the subconscious mind (Lesson Five). But these methods can also be used to access information in the Universal Mind. Many cases are reported in *Power vs. Force,* and an extensive bibliography of books containing more examples is given in *The Pendulum Kit,* by Lonegren (Appendix A.)

- Many cases of lost animals that found their way home have been reported and verified. One confirmed case was about a family that moved from Ohio to Oregon with their pet dog. The dog was lost in Indiana. The family stayed several days in Indiana but could not find the dog. They proceeded to their new home in Oregon. Two months later their dog showed up. The dog had never been to Oregon before.

The path of the dog was traced by a reporter. The reporter placed ads in newspapers to find witnesses who saw the dog along the route. He found that the dog's route was almost a direct line. The dog could not find its family over a thousand miles away by odor, memory, or magnetic forces. The route to his master's home had to come from intelligence outside of the dog's mind, a higher intelligence.

Rupert Sheldrake, a reputable English scientist, has studied many such cases and conducted scientific experiments on animals. His studies show that pets with a strong attachment to their owners react to the owner's thoughts, even when the owners are away from home. How can these pets do that unless there is some intelligent field that is common to the pet and owner? Many examples are reported in his books.

- A consequential discovery in quantum physics is the phenomenon of *entanglement*. Einstein referred to it as "spooky action at a distance." Briefly, when two or more particles react with each other (become entangled) and are then separated, each continues to react to the other when either is subjected to a force. They react regardless of the distance between them, and the response time is ten million times the speed of light. That is to say, they react as *they are really parts of one system*.

  Entanglement is based on a theory by J. S. Bell that has been verified experimentally several times. [2]

- Intercessory prayer is when the person praying and the person being prayed for are apart. Distance has no effect on results. When you think about it, most

---

[2] Aczel, Amir D., *Entanglement, The Greatest Mystery In Physics,* Four Walls Eight Windows, 2001.

prayer fits this description. The prayor and the prayee are seldom touching even if they are in the same room. So what is the medium that transports prayer from person to person? There has to be a field of higher intelligence that is common to both parties.

Now you have the concept of Universal Mind. I want to point out one more reason the information from the preceding lessons applies to the Universal Mind as well.

AS ABOVE, SO BELOW

A law is valid in the vertical as well as the horizontal direction. That is, if a law is valid on one level of consciousness, it has to be valid on all levels. A law is universal. So if the laws discussed in the previous seven lessons are correct, they must be correct at this higher level of mind as well. A law could not work one way in the conscious mind and subconscious mind and another way in the Universal Mind. So if the laws discussed in the previous eight lessons are valid, they are valid for prayer as well.

There are four *key* concepts carried over from the previous lessons that are critical for making your prayers more effective. They are: 1) Pray in the Alpha/Theta States, 2) Be Affirmative, 3) Be Single-Minded, and 4) Make Your Subconscious Mind Faith Full.

KEY NO. 1: PRAY IN THE ALPHA STATE

Praying in the alpha (and/or theta state) makes prayers more effective—hundreds, if not thousands, of times more effective. When praying in the beta state your brain waves are diffused and unfocused. The energy is scattered. When praying in the alpha state, your brain waves are focused and more powerful. Think of the difference between an

Incandescent light bulb and a laser beam. The incandescent bulb emits light in all directions and wastes most of the energy as heat. All the energy in a laser beam is focused and it is so powerful that it can burn through steel. All of the waves in a laser beam are in sync and their energy is added exponentially. That is why lasers are so powerful.

There is yet another reason for praying in the alpha state of mind. I propose that the subconscious mind plays a large part in prayer. Thus, you need to be in the alpha state to access your subconscious mind.

UNDIRECTED ENERGY

Conscious mind supplies the will, shows the intent, and couches the words in a prayer. But the subconscious mind supplies the passion, i.e., the energy. In some way the subconscious mind is an important link to the Universal Mind.

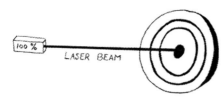

LASER BEAM

DIRECTED ENERGY

Possibly prayer is amplified by the subconscious mind as it passes through the subconscious mind to get to the Universal Mind. Whatever the mechanism is, the subconscious mind adds the power and plays a critical part in successful prayer.

Consider this circumstantial evidence to support the above theory.

- As described earlier, dogs have access to the Universal Mind, and dogs do not have a conscious mind, at least not one anywhere near as developed as in humans. This implies the conscious mind is not critical for accessing the Universal Mind.

- Education is not a factor in prayer. A person with a Ph.D. is not necessarily better at praying because of his or her education, even if it is in religion. A person with a degree or position in religion is probably better, but only because of experience and passion. It is noteworthy that Eastern practices of healing, prayer, or meditation, teach getting the educated mind (conscious mind) out of the way. Success in prayer comes from the heart (subconscious mind), not from the intellect (conscious mind).

- I propose that devout religious persons are better at prayer because, when they pray, they naturally go into the alpha state. This is because they have been exposed to, and trained in procedures that teach going into alpha automatically. Such procedures include: quietude, relaxation, slowed breathing, altruistic passion, emotion, rituals, meditation, and repeating a simple prayer over and over (rosary beads, chanting, and drumming). Also, their intent is probably more altruistic than the average lay person.

- Emotion is very important, maybe the most import, factor in prayer and emotion comes from the subconscious mind. The logical conscious mind tends to inhibit emotion. Dossey found that love and compassion were strong forces in prayer.

- Scientists recently found that when highly religious people prayed or meditated, they exhibited intense

theta brain waves. This study implies going in deep theta state of mind is even better than the alpha state.

• At another facility, scientists studied subjects who have deep religious experiences during prayer or meditation[3]. Among these subjects were nuns and Buddhists. The scientists made several surprising observations when the subjects had their peak religious experiences. There is a small area in the back of the subconscious mind that constantly calculates spatial orientation—the sense of where one's body ends and the world begins. During intense prayer or meditation, this area becomes "a quiet oasis of inactivity." And in a related article published in *Psychiatry Research,* "...they have a complete dissolving of the self, and sense of union, a sense of infinite spacelessness." This area is in the subconscious mind.

In each case above, the key to successful praying was the subconscious mind, not the conscious mind.

KEY NO. 2: USE AFFIRMATIVE PRAYER

Many prayers are an affirmation of something desired. A prayer can be, for example, for a physical healing for yourself or someone else, better job, or bringing more loving relationships into your life. Thus, your affirmative prayer should be based on the same rules outlined in Lesson Eight. Take a minute and go back to Lesson Eight and review the section on affirmations.

Importantly, the subconscious mind and the Universal Mind do not operate in the same time frame your conscious

---

[3] *Boston Globe,* May 13, 2001

mind does. So your affirmative prayer must be stated in the *present* tense. You must talk, see, feel, and act as if you *already have* the results you are praying for. If you pray for better health but think and visualize yourself as being sick, *being sick* is what your subconscious mind projects to the Universal Mind. And the Universal Mind will grant your prayer—being sick.

The second most important point is to use emotion. According to some studies in the scientific literature, the most import factors in prayer are expressing *love* and *compassion.* Interestingly, results of some studies show that when you pray for someone else, your prayer does as much, or more, good for you as it does for the person you are praying for.

The above is essential but the following are only suggestions that you might find helpful.

Rather than to start a prayer right off with an affirmation, establish a rapport with God. Just like when you talk to your subconscious mind, you should be friendly and courteous. Start with a greeting. This helps enrich your connection with God. You might use this part of your prayer to just pay homage to God.

Then you need to tune in to the Universal Mind. Tune in by acknowledging that the Universal Mind is all-knowing, has the answer to your prayer, and is available to you.

Then give your affirmative prayer.

After that, like any good, considerate person, say, "Thank you." Be profusely thankful for the result, which you are already visualizing as fulfilled. Be thankful, not only for this result, but for *all* your blessings.

Then let it go. The Universal Mind knows how to do it better than you. Using your conscious mind is counterproductive.

KEY NO. 3: BE SINGLE-MINDED

Your subconscious mind can hold many concepts on a subject, but it will only hold one of them as binding. And that concept will dominate your subconscious mind. This law was discussed in Lesson Four. Thus, when you pray for something, it is imperative that your subconscious mind holds the same truth about that something as your conscious mind.

For example, suppose his doctor tells Frank that he has a weak heart. Immediately Frank starts praying—in the present tense—that he has a strong, healthy heart. Frank's conscious mind accepts the idea that he already has a strong healthy heart. But suppose the dominant concept in his subconscious mind is that he has a *weak* heart. (That dominant thought in the subconscious mind may be the cause of the weak heart in the first place.)

That "weak heart" concept could have originated from an incident such as this. Frank witnessed a relative die from a heart attack when he was three years old. The situation was highly emotional. Frank's conscious mind has forgotten the incident but his subconscious mind has not. The incident was traumatic and left a strong impression in his subconscious mind, so strong that it dominated.

Further assume that Frank's mother, who he had a strong emotional bond with and who was sobbing uncontrollably, said (or three-year-old Frank thought she said) "Weak hearts run in our family. Our child will have a weak heart too." From then on, Frank's subconscious mind accepted the idea that he had a weak heart. Even though Frank had no conscious reason to believe his heart was weak, the concept in his subconscious mind dominated. (When conscious mind and subconscious mind are in conflict, subconscious mind always wins.)

Now, in Frank's prayers, the subconscious mind dominates the conscious mind and his prayers go unanswered.

Frank's prayers will be ineffective due to this internal conflict.

Frank must program his *subconscious* mind to accept the idea that he has a strong, hale, healthy heart. As soon as his conscious mind and subconscious mind are in sync, in harmony in the belief that he has a strong heart, which is the truth, his affirmative prayer will be sent to the Universal Mind and it will be answered.

When you pray for something, condition your subconscious mind (as explained in Lesson Eight) to accept the concept as truth, just as it is in your conscious mind. Then your conscious mind and subconscious mind will work together "single-mindedly" in harmony to ensure success of your prayer.

KEY NO. 4: MAKE YOUR SUBCONSCIOUS MIND FAITH FULL

Faith is universally accepted as crucial for successful prayer. The importance of faith is found throughout the New Testament and I imagine, the Koran, Torah, etc. It is the foundation of healing and successful prayer. When your prayers do not work, it may be due to lack of faith. You may think you have faith and sincerely believe in your religious doctrines. But that is your conscious mind you are talking about. What does your subconscious mind hold as truth?

Your faith is not complete if it is only instilled in your conscious mind: faith must also be ingrained in your subconscious mind. Unless you were exposed to nothing but the doctrines of your religion and the rules from the preceding lessons from the time you were born (and you believed and accepted them!), the concepts in your subconscious mind probably do not coincide with those in your conscious mind. These concepts need to be in concert in your conscious mind and subconscious mind for maximum prayer power. You need to be single-minded in your faith.

To overcome this lack of, or contrary faith in your subconscious mind, you need to program your subconscious mind with the beliefs in your conscious mind. Until the concepts in your conscious mind and subconscious mind are in agreement, these conflicting beliefs could be the cause of unsuccessful prayers.

There is another reason faith is crucial. Recall in Lesson Four where I pointed out that if you entertain doubt, i.e., any *fear* of failure, you will likely fail. Fear is in the subconscious mind and if it is stronger than your *will* to succeed, you will fail. So any fear may weaken your prayer. You need a strong enough faith to override any fear of failure.

This brings up an important point. Prayer works and it is capable of anything. Prayer has no limits. But, if you pray for something that you know (conscious mind) and feel (subconscious mind) is not possible, you will entertain a fear of failure, a fear that you may not be able to overcome.

For example, suppose Mary is diagnosed with a form of fatal cancer. There is hope. Spontaneous remission of cancers has been documented. Elmer and Alyce Green investigated over 400 cases of spontaneous remission years ago, and there are many more cases on record since then. So it is *possible* that Mary could have a spontaneous remission and wake up the next day with no trace of cancer.

If Mary prays for complete recovery by tomorrow, unless she is superhuman, she will have strong doubts about it. She will entertain some fear that it might not happen. This fear will weaken and probably defeat her prayer.

But she could pray without reservation for the start of healing. She could pray without reservation for her immune system to kick in to a higher gear and start killing the cancer cells *now*. She could pray without reservation to be stronger tomorrow than she is today and for her healthy cells to multiply and crowd out the cancerous cells *now*. She could

pray for a lot of things that she could have complete confidence in. My suggestion is to pray for things you can be confident in achieving. Miracles do not have to be instantaneous; it is okay if they take a little time.

Prayer works. If it is not working for you, maybe lack of faith in your subconscious mind is blocking your prayer. Write a long affirmation about every aspect of your beliefs, and what you want to have faith in, and instill that affirmation in your subconscious mind so that is the only truth it holds.

CONCLUSIONS

Put a thousand times more ooooph in your prayers:

- Pray in the alpha, or better yet, theta state of mind.

- Use affirmative prayer. Visualize the result, not the problem.

- Feel and express love and compassion.

- Be certain you are single-minded: be absolutely certain your conscious mind and subconscious mind are in agreement.

- Program your subconscious mind for strong, fervent faith to coincide with that in your conscious mind.

- Be thankful and express gratitude for all blessings.

[Handwritten notes:]

I have great looking full head of hair

I have beautiful clear skin

I have great TALL positive

I look great with great style and good looks

I love to work
I love to work out
I love to stay healthy Diet

I AM so SUCCESSFUL
I MAKE $400,000 per year

I AM so FIT AND HEALTHY
I AM muscular and thin
I have a 6 pack stomach
I weigh 165 lbs with 6% body fat

I AM so OUTGOING CHARISMATIC and confident

WONDERFUL THINGS HAPPEN TO ME EVERY DAY AND NIGHT

APPENDIX A

BIBLIOGRAPHY AND SUGGESTED READING

Lessons One through Eight

Achterberg, Jeanne, *Imagery in Healing: Shamanism and Modern Medicine,* New Science Library, 1985.

Andersen, U.S., *Three Magic Words,* Thomas elson & sons, 1954.

Bailes, Frederick, W., *Your Mind Can Heal You,* Dodd, Mead, 1941.

Bristol, Claude M., *The Magic of Believing,* A Pocket Book, 1969.

Brooks, Harry C., *The Practice of Autosuggestion by the Method of Emile Coué,* Dodd, Mead and Co., 1922.

Borysenko, Joan, Ph.D., *Minding The Body, Mending The Mind,* Bantam Books, 1988.

Cantor, Alfred J., M.D., *Unitrol: The Healing Magic of the Mind,* Parker Publishing Company, Inc., 1965.

Chopra, Deepak, M.D., *Ageless Body, Timeless Mind,* Harmony Books, 1993.

Chopra, Deepak, M.D., *Creating Health,* Houghton Mifflin Company, 1987.

Chopra, Deepak, M.D., *The Seven Spiritual Laws of Success,* Amber-Allen Publishing, 1994.

Collier, Robert, *The Secret of the Ages,* Robert Collier Publications, Inc., 1948

Dossey, Larry, M.D., *Meaning & Medicine,* Bantam Books, 1991.

Dossey, Larry, M.D., *Recovering The Soul,* A Bantam Book, 1989.

Duckworth, John, *How To Use Auto-Suggestion Effectively,* Wilshire Book Company, 1966

Dyer, Wayne W., *Manifest Your Destiny,* Harper Collins, 1997.

Gallwey, W. Timothy, *The Inner Game of Tennis,* Random House, Inc. 1974.

Germain, Walter M., *The Magic Power of Your Mind,* Hawthorn Books, Inc., 1956.

Green, Elmer & Alyce, Beyond Biofeedback, Delta, 1977.

Hawkings, David R., M.D., Ph.D., *Power vs. Force,* Hay House, inc., 2002.

Hawkings, David R., M.D., Ph.D., *The Eye of the I,* Veritas, 2001.

Helmstetter, Shad, Ph.D., *What To Say When You Talk To Your Self,* Pocket Books, 1986.

Howard, Vernon, *Psychho-Pictography,* Parker Publishing Company, Inc., 1965.

King, Serge, *Imagineering for Health,* A quest Book, 1981.

Lecron, Leslie M., *Magic Mind Power,* DeVoss & Company, 1969.

Lecron, Leslie M, *Self-Hypnotism: The Technique and Its Use in Daily Living,* Prentice-Hall, Inc, 1964.

Lonegren, Sig, *The Pendulum Kit*, Simon &Schuster, 1990.

Maltz, Maxwell, M.D., *The Magic Power of Self-Image Psychology,* Prentice-Hall, Inc., 1964.

Maltz, Maxwell, M.D., *Psycho-Cybernetics,* Prentice-Hall, Inc., 1960.

Murphy, Joseph, D.D., D.R.S., Ph.D., L.L., *The Power of Your Subconscious Mind,* Prentice-Hall, Inc., 1963.

Murphy, Joseph, D.D., D.R.S., Ph.D., L.L.D., *The Amazing Laws of Cosmic Mind Power,* Paperback Library Edition, 1969.

Peale, Norman Vincent, *How To Make Positive Imaging Work For You,* Foundation for Christian Living, Pawling, NY, 1982.

Peale, Norman Vincent, *The Power of Positive Thinking,* Prentice-Hall, Inc. 1954

Pelletier, Kenneth R., *Mind as Healer: Mind as Slayer,* Delta, 1977.

Pert, Candice, Ph.D., *Molecules of Emotion*, Scribner & Sons, 1997.

Sanders Jr., Pete A., *Access Your Brain's Joy Center,* Mission Possible Printing, 1996.

Siegel, Bernie S., M.D., *Love, Medicine & Miracles,* Harper & Row, Publishers, 1986.

Siegel, Bernie S., M.D., *Peace, Love & Healing,* Harper & Row, Publishers, 1989.

Simonton, Carl O., and Stephanie Matthews-Simonton, and L. Creighton, *Getting Well Again,* Bantam, 1992.

Sarno, John E., M.D., *Healing Back Pain,* Warner Books, 1991

Steadman, Alice, *Who's the Matter With Me?* DeVorss Publications, 1966.

Takus, James A., *Your Mind Can Drive You Crazy,* Psychonetix, Inc., Tarzana, CA, 1978.

Williams, John K., *The Knack of Using Your Subconscious Mind,* Prentice-Hall, Inc. 1971.

APPENDIX B

BIBLIOGRAPHY AND SUGGESTED READING

Lesson on Prayer

Anderson, U.S., *Three Magic Words,* Wilshire Book Company, 1970.

Capra, Fritjof, *The Tao of Physics,* Sambhala Publications, Inc., 1980.

Dossey, Larry, M.D., *Healing Words, The Power of Prayer and The Practice of Medicine,* HarperSanFrancisco, 1993.

Dossey, Larry, M.D., *Prayer Is Good Medicine,* HarperCollins Publishers, *1996*

Dossey, Larry, M.D., *Be Careful What You Pray For...You Just Might Get It,* HarperSanFrancisco, 1997.

Dyer, Wayne W., *There's A Spiritual Solution to Every Problem,* HarperCollins, 2001

Hawkins, David R., M.D., Ph.D., *Power Vs. Force,* Hay House, Inc. 2002.

Lonegren, Sig, *The Pendulum Kit,* Simon & Schuster, 1990.

Sheldrake, Rupert, *Dogs That Know When Their Owners Are Coming Home,* Crown, 1999.

Silva, Jose, *The Silva Mind Control Method,* Simon and Schuster, 1977.

Talbot, Michael, *Beyond the Quantum,* Bantam, 1988.

Zukav, Gary, *The Dancing Wu Li Masters,* Bantam Books, 1986.

"Power of suggestion"

get "IT works"

Women are from VENUS
Men are from MARS

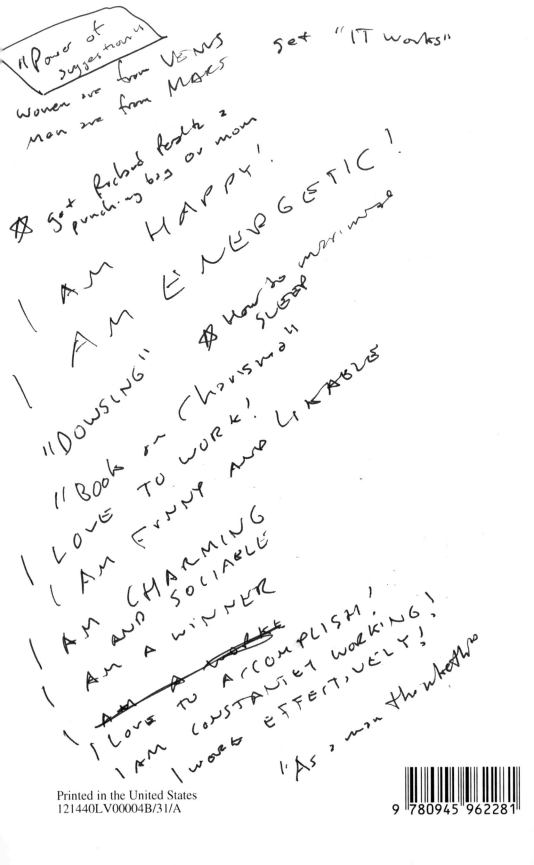

✡ get Richard Restak's punching bag or more

I AM HAPPY!

I AM ENERGETIC!

✡ How to maximize sleep

"DOWSING"

"Book on Charisma"

I LOVE TO WORK!

I AM FUNNY AND LIKABLE

I AM CHARMING AND SOCIABLE

I AM A WINNER

I LOVE TO ACCOMPLISH!

I AM CONSTANTLY WORKING!

I work EFFECTIVELY!

"AS a man thinketh"

Printed in the United States
121440LV00004B/31/A

9 780945 962281